In the Household of the Spirit:

A Western Christian's Guide to the Sacraments
in the Byzantine Church

by

B.J. Lawrence Cross

and

Joseph H.J. Leach

Published in 2014 by

Freedom Publishing Company Pty Ltd
35 Whitehorse Rd, Balwyn, Melbourne, Victoria 3103, Australia

Telephone: (61 3) 9816 0820
Fax: (61 3) 9816 0899

Email: books@freedompublishing.com.au
Website: www.freedompublishing.com.au

Printer: Brougham Press
33 Scoresby Rd, Bayswater Victoria 3153, Australia

Cover design and layout: Manark Printing
28 Dingley Avenue, Dandenong, Victoria 3175

Spirit and Fire:
A Western Christian's Guide to the Sacraments in the Byzantine Church

ISBN 978-0-9775699-9-1

CONTENTS

Introduction

I am only a man. I need visible signs. I tire easily building the stairway of abstraction.

Czeslaw Milosz

Arise, and let my voice be heard.,

Charged with my will go forth and span

The land and sea, and let my word

Lay waste with fire the heart of man

Pushkin

In all its most ancient traditions Christianity is a sacramental religion. Sacraments form the very life of the Church through which the Spirit of God flows into the world. However, sacramentality implies a particular view of nature which is radically at odds with the secular, materialist view of modern western culture – a view that holds creation to be graced, sacred and full of meaning. The sacredness of nature thus lies at the very heart of Christianity and it is vital, when our relationship with nature is looming as one of the great moral questions of our time, that we understand how fundamental the sacredness of nature is to the sacramental life of the Church. In recent times this has become difficult in the Western Church because of the minimalist and informal way in which the liturgy and the sacraments are often approached. A study of the Eastern Church, with its love of solemn ritual and symbol, can perhaps lead Western Christians back to an appreciation of the full richness and grandeur of Christian sacramental life. It is hoped that such a study will awaken a renewed love of the liturgy and the sacraments in the life of the Western Church.

In our modern world the very idea of a sacrament needs some explanation. Traditional societies understood them better. In traditional societies the world was defined by human and sacred values. The divine was seen as close in the natural world, while the affairs of the natural world and those of the human world were seen as intertwined. It was in the natural world and in life that people met their God. Modern western culture, on the other hand, views the universe as a three dimensional grid of space/time extending to infinity and independent of human existence or perception. Since the sacred and the divine can not be measured nor confined within such a universe, this utilitarian, reductionist view has no place for them. They do not fit. Even such human values as beauty and love are seen as purely cultural or biological artefacts with no objective reality. In such a view of the universe human life itself, indeed all life, can only be considered as an incidental and unimportant accident. Descriptions of this view are well known to all of us from the populist astronomy books we read as children or from "educational" television programs. A typical example would read something like this: we are a species of ape living on a small planet orbiting one very average star among billions of stars, on the outskirts of one galaxy among billions of galaxies. The clear message, either implicit or explicit, is that there is nothing special about us and that it is foolish to attach any significance to human existence – or even to existence itself. This is often stated not as opinion or as philosophical viewpoint, but as if it were fact

"...the universe is, to say the least, utterly indifferent to us. In the words of a 16th century tanka (a Japanese verse-form) we are 'no more than fleeting foam on the surface of a violent sea.'"[1]

This has been even more bluntly, and less poetically, stated by the Cambridge physicist Prof. Stephen Hawking:

"The human race is just a chemical scum on a moderate-sized planet.[2]"

This radical reductionist view of reality and humanity's place within it, is not the traditional view of European culture, nor is it some natural, underlying view of reality which has been obscured in the past by human religion and culture – a kind of "default" or "natural" view. Although its adherents often treat such a world view as supra-cultural in this way, this reductionist view is clearly the product of the specific history and culture of 16th and 17th century Europe[3]. It is a view that has developed with the attempted application of empirical, scientific methodology to the concepts of human society and existence, even though this methodology cannot be properly applied in these areas. It is a product of the triumphal anthropocentrism of the industrial revolution[4]. In its most basic form it is a view that holds that only that which can be objectively observed and measured truly exists. It is ironic that a world view which holds the mind of man to be the final authority in the universe also denies any fundamental significance to human existence.

Not only does such a view give our society problems when conversing with the remaining, meaning-rich traditional societies, it also means that many in western society live out their lives in a hostile, indifferent universe they believe to be devoid of meaning or beauty.

This malaise is well expressed by Alain de Botton, English writer and philosopher, in his reflections on a visit to the Westminster branch of Mac Donald's.

---

1   Heidmann, J. 1995. *Extra terrestrial Intelligence* Cambridge University Press, Cambridge. P3.
2   as quoted in Davies, P. 2006, *The Goldilocks Enigma*, Allen Lane, London.
3   Szerszynski, B. 2006, Keynote Address, *Critical Perspectives on Religion and the Environment*, Subject Centre for Philosophical and Religious Studies, University of Leeds.
4   Cf. *"Not even God could sink the Titanic!"*

The mood inside the restaurant was solemn and concentrated. Customers were eating alone, reading papers or staring at the brown tiles, masticating with a sternness and brusqueness beside which the atmosphere of a feeding shed would have seemed convivial and mannered. The setting served to render all kinds of ideas absurd: that human beings might sometimes be generous to one another without hope of reward; that relationships can on occasion be sincere; that life may be worth enduring... The harsh lighting, the intermittent sound of frozen fries being sunk into vats of oil and the frenzied behaviour of the counter staff invited thoughts of the loneliness and meaninglessness of existence in a random and violent universe[5].

This sense of meaninglessness is exacerbated by a lack of historical consciousness which means that many people tend to regard the current secular, humanist view of the world as the view that is the 'natural' default view underlying, and independent of, all human culture - the view that is "objectively true" and "scientifically correct". This is the view used by atheistic groups as a weapon against the traditional religions all of which ascribe a deep significance, not only to human life, but to the whole of the cosmos. It is clear from the drop in religious practice in many western countries that over the course of the twentieth century this attack began to have some effect. The rise of this world view also coincides with the development of the utilitarian view of nature, a view which sees the natural world primarily as a resource for commercial exploitation. This has caused massive environmental degradation.

Ironically, what has replaced the traditional religions, with their reasoned theology, was not rational, secular humanism, but the superstition of the New Age movement and more bizarre sects. This was inevitable since the reductionist view of the world has no place for those very things which make human life rich and full. We are sacramental by nature, always seeking meaning and purpose in the things around us. This is one of the things which defines us as human beings. Indeed, cognitive science tells us that even our eyes work not so much to see what is, but as to see the meaning of what is. The ultimate failure of the secular, reductionist view of the universe is that it can not adequately describe human life as it is lived and experienced.

Of course, value laden reductionist descriptions, such as the one given above, do not even accurately represent the understanding of science. We live around an average star not because we are mediocre or insignificant, but because any other type of star would give either too much or too little radiation. Similarly, we live on the edge of the galaxy because those stars closer to the galaxy's core are all deadly to life, either because of more frequent bursts of radiation from super novas or because of disastrous stellar close encounters. In short, we seem to live on a planet orbiting the only kind of star which could support life. Moreover, we live on a planet which is

---

5   Alain de Botton 2006, *The Architecture of Happiness*, Penguin, London.

remarkable in many ways; it has oceans of liquid water, it has a large iron core and a strong consequent magnetic field, which protects the surface from solar radiation, it has a large moon which gives tides to the oceans etc. Many of these features are the result of an extremely unlikely collision about four billion years ago, a collision so unlikely that the Earth is probably unique in the galaxy. This collision, between the proto-earth and a Mars sized planetoid, profoundly effected the subsequent development of the planet. So, we live on a very unusual, possibly unique, planet and it is those very features that make it so unusual which also make it an ideal home for life. To describe it as an average sized planet, implying that it itself is average, is simply not accurate.

Even the very constants which define the physical nature of our universe have just those values which make life possible. If any of these constants had had other values then matter, stars, planets and biochemical reactions would have been impossible. All of this has led physicist Paul Davies to comment "*the universe seems like a put up job*"[6]. In a later book Davies has called this the *Goldilocks Enigma*[7]. Why do we live in a universe where the very laws of physics are, like Goldilocks' porridge, "just right" for life? Reflecting on this, Davies writes:

"*I cannot accept these features as a package of marvels which just happen to be, which exist reasonlessly. It seems to me that there is a genuine scheme of things – the universe is about something*[8]."

It is worth noting that this is not a view which comes from a religious standpoint, Davies is not a Christian, but rather from a mature reflection on scientific knowledge. It is a view of the world which is more "scientific" than the "humanity as chemical scum" view described above. Reductionist thinking has no adequate explanation for human life as it is experienced nor even for the features of the universe in which we live. We live in a universe which seems to be designed to bring forth life and we are a part of that universe. We are, indeed, that universe conscious of itself.

Given the failure of the secular humanist view of reality to provide an adequate framework for an understanding of human life, it may well be time to look at an earlier view of the universe; one which was not so much concerned with how the universe worked but more with where it came from and where it was going – not so much with what it was but with the meaning of what it was. This is the view of reality expressed in the sacramental life of the Christian Church where all of creation is seen as sacramental – a symbol which mediates the thing that it symbolizes, an efficacious sign of the grace and love of God. Indeed, Paul Collins was expressing a very ancient and traditional Christian view when he said that

---

6   Davies, P. *The Mind of God*
7   Davies, P. 2006, *The Goldilocks Enigma*, Allen Lane, London.
8   Ibid

creation was the "primal sacrament of God"[9]. The sacramentality of nature and its role in the sacramental life of the Church was emphasized by Pope John Paul II:

Christianity does not reject matter. Rather, bodiliness is considered in all its value in the liturgical act, whereby the human body is disclosed in its inner nature as a temple of the Spirit and is united with the Lord Jesus, who himself took a body for the world's salvation. This does not mean, however, an absolute exaltation of all that is physical, for we know well the chaos which sin introduced into the harmony of the human being. The liturgy reveals that the body, through the mystery of the Cross, is in the process of transfiguration, pneumatization: on Mount Tabor Christ showed his body radiant, as the Father wants it to be again. Cosmic reality also is summoned to give thanks because the whole universe is called to recapitulation in Christ the Lord. This concept expresses a balanced and marvelous teaching on the dignity, respect and purpose of creation and of the human body in particular. With the rejection of all dualism and every cult of pleasure as an end in itself, the body becomes a place made luminous by grace and thus fully human. To those who seek a truly meaningful relationship with themselves and with the cosmos, so often disfigured by selfishness and greed, the liturgy reveals the way to the harmony of the new man, and invites him to respect the Eucharistic potential of the created world. That world is destined to be assumed in the Eucharist of the Lord, in his Passover, present in the sacrifice of the altar[10].

Christianity has had a sacramental view of creation from its very earliest beginnings. In its battle against the Manicheans, an early Middle Eastern sect who saw all matter as evil, the Church proclaimed that creation is good, an efficacious symbol of the love and grace of God and is destined to enter, through the priesthood of Christ, into the very life of the triune God. In the Christian view, the world we see around us is not only sacred but is also the vehicle for the grace of God. If this was not true of creation, then our sacramental rituals would be empty play acting. But it is true. Nature is graced and sacred from its creation by God and the grace of its creation, while it can be obscured by sin and evil, can never be destroyed. Evgueny Lampert put this well:

Nature is symbolic, and the power of this symbolism is the mystery of the life of Nature. The Holy Spirit came down into the world at its creation; His everlasting presence is its very life, and Nature witnesses to Him...Whence does the world of Nature receive its power of life, of growth, of development if not from the divine 'fiat' resounding in its very depths? This 'fiat' is the call of the divine Spirit to Nature to be, or to become what it already is in its inner destiny and meaning. Nature has never ceased to be a symbol; and the power of the Holy Spirit, which is also the power of cosmic beauty, of life and being, will never die away from the

9   Collins, P. 1995, *God's Earth*, Harper Collins, Australia.
10   Pope John Paul II in his apostolic letter *Orientale Lumen, 1995.*

depths of her immensity: 'et vidit Deus quod esset bonum'![11]

This is the ancient understanding of the Christian Church, both east and west, and each branch of the Church has sought to express this sacramental understanding in its own cultural and historical circumstances. This understanding pervades Christian life. It is expressed not only in the great sacraments of the Church but also in the small sacraments of prayer and Christian living which incorporate the sacred in day to day life. Some ancient and beautiful examples of this are the prayers of the people of the Hebrides Islands which were collected and translated by Alexander Carmichael in the nineteenth century[12]. Many of these prayers have at their core a powerful understanding of the sacred in nature. The following is but one example:

There is no plant in the ground

But is full of his virtue.

There is no form in the strand

But is full of his blessing....

There is no life in the sea

There is no creature in the river

There is naught in the firmament

But proclaims his goodness...

There is no bird on the wing,

There is no star in the sky,

There is nothing beneath the sun

But proclaims his goodness...[13].

These prayers arise from a sacramental view of the world, a world suffused with the grace and love of God. It is a world view as warm as the rationalist view is cold, as profound as the rationalist view is superficial, and as full of meaning and hope as the rationalist view is pointless and despairing. This world view was not a peculiar product of the Hebrides Islands nor even of Gaelic Culture, though the way in which it was expressed certainly was. Rather it is a view that was once the

11   Evgeny Lampert, The Divine Realm: Towards a theology of the Sacraments, London: 1943, Faber and Faber Ltd, p115.

12   Carmicael, A. 1899. *Carmina Gadelica: Hymns and Incantations from the Gaelic.* Floris Books (New edition 2004) 684pp.

13   ibid

common wisdom of all Christians and even, to some extent, of all humanity. Esther De Waal describes the world and way of life from which these prayers arose in the following way:

"...(they had) prayers whose daily and yearly rhythms marked their lives: prayers from birth to death, from dawn to dusk, from the start of the year to its close, for they lived quite naturally in a state of prayer. It was a praying which responded to, and grew out of, their way of life ...grew out of their sense of the presence of God as the most immediate reality in their lives. Religion permeated everything they did. They made no distinctions between the secular and the sacred. They were unable to discern boundaries of where religion began and ended and thus found it natural to assume that God was lovingly concerned in everything they did. They felt totally at home with God[14]."

What is said here of the people of the Hebrides Islands could also be said of the peasant in the great Russian spiritual classic *The Way of a Pilgrim[15]*, an anonymous story from the mid-nineteenth century which tells the tale of a peasant pilgrim on a journey to visit the shrine of St. Innocent in Irkutsk, and thence onto Jerusalem. Consider the following passages:

"...everything around me seemed delightful and marvelous. The trees, the grass, the birds, the earth, the air, the light seemed to be telling me that they existed for man's sake, that they witnessed to the love of God for man, that all things prayed to God and sang His praise."[16]

and

"...the whole outside world also seemed to me to be full of charm and delight. Everything drew me to love and thank God: people, trees, plants, animals. I saw them all as my kinsfolk. I found on all of them the magic name of Jesus."[17]

What the simple fishing and farming people from the Hebrides Islands to Siberia and beyond expressed in their daily prayers, the great minds, the engineers, architects and artists of Christendom sought to express not just in ritual but in stone – in simple parish Churches as much as in great cathedrals. Their efforts have sometimes been endearing and sometimes awe-inspiring but they have always attempted to express a view of the world that is diametrically opposed to the empty reductionist view of the modern secular world. The great cathedrals of Europe express a world view which sees nature as sacred and full of meaning, pregnant with the grace of God, transformed by the incarnation of Christ and destined, at the culmination of time, to transcend its limitations and be joined to the divine. How well they succeeded

---

14 De Waal, E. 1988, *The Celtic Vision*, Darton, Longman and Todd, London.
15 Billy, D.J. (Trans.) 2000. *The Way of a Pilgrim: complete text and reader's guide*. Ligouri Press, Missouri.
16 Ibid, p49
17 Ibid, p145

can be judged by contrasting Alain de Botton's reflections on a visit to Westminster Cathedral with those of his visit to the Westminster MacDonald's:

The facile din of the outer world had given way to awe and silence...Everything serious in human nature seemed to be called to the surface: thoughts about limits and infinity, about powerlessness and sublimity. The stonework threw into relief all that was compromised and dull and kindled a yearning to live up to its perfections. After about ten minutes in the cathedral, a range of ideas that would have been inconceivable outside began to assume an air of reasonableness. Under the influence of the marble, the mosaics, the darkness, and the incense, it seemed entirely probable that Jesus was the Son of God and has walked across the Sea of Galilee...

Touring the cathedrals today with cameras and guidebooks in hand, we may experience something at odds with our practical secularism: a peculiar and embarrassing desire to fall on our knees and worship a being as mighty and sublime as we ourselves are small and inadequate[18].

This communication of the sacred in the things of this world is at the core of any understanding of the sacraments. Assaulted by the secularism of our age, many Western Christians have to some degree lost their sensitivity to the sacramental rituals of the Church and may now need to look to their brothers and sisters of the Eastern Church to regain the fullness of sacramental understanding. Long before the split began to open between the two Churches, begining in the eleventh century[19], each of the Churches had developed its own culture and ecclesiastical style. In theology the West was more analytical and the East more mystical (although both Churches knew both analytical and mystical theology). In liturgical practice, the West favored simplicity and directness while the East valued beauty and elaboration. Neither approach is wrong, neither really excludes the other, and each has its strengths. Legitimate diversity is the glory of God, as Pope John Paul II has pointed out:

From the beginning, the Christian East has proved to contain a wealth of forms capable of assuming the characteristic features of each individual culture, with supreme respect for each particular community. We can only thank God with deep emotion for the wonderful variety with which he has allowed such a rich and composite mosaic of different tesserae to be formed[20].

However, in this minimalist, post-modern age, Pope John Paul II recognized that Western Christians now had to learn the wisdom of their Eastern brothers and

---

18   Alain de Botton 2006, *The Architecture of Happiness*, Penguin, London.
19   The circumstances of the split are complicated and beyond the scope of this book. Bishop Kallistos Ware has an
     excellent discussion on this topic in his book *The Orthodox Church*, Penguin, London, 1963.
20   Pope John Paul II in his apostolic letter *Orientale Lumen, 1995.*

sisters and so appreciate the fullness and richness of God's Church.

Within this framework, liturgical prayer in the East shows a great aptitude for involving the human person in his or her totality: the mystery is sung in the loftiness of its content, but also in the warmth of the sentiments it awakens in the heart of redeemed humanity. In the sacred act, even bodiliness is summoned to praise, and beauty, which in the East is one of the best loved names expressing the divine harmony and the model of humanity transfigured, appears everywhere: in the shape of the Church, in the sounds, in the colours, in the lights, in the scents. The lengthy duration of the celebrations, the repeated invocations, everything expresses gradual identification with the mystery celebrated with one's whole person. Thus the prayer of the Church already becomes participation in the heavenly liturgy, an anticipation of the final beatitude[21].

This is not to say that Western Christians should abandon their own liturgical and sacramental practice and traditions but rather that they should use the sacramental understanding of the Eastern Church to enhance their understanding of their own sacraments, to appreciate fully the depth of symbolic meaning and to live the Christian life in all its fullness. It is by coming to know the East that the West can learn to understand itself.

In one of his Narnia books, *The Voyage of the Dawn Treader*, C.S. Lewis has one of his child heroes in conversation with a magician about the nature of stars. The boy repeats what he has been taught at school, that stars are just big balls of flaming gas. The magician says that that is not true in Narnia (in Narnia stars are people and the magician himself turns out to be a former star) but also points out that even in our own world that is not what stars are but only what they are made of. A reductionist view sees everything as only being what it is made of. A sacramental view goes beyond this superficial understanding and sees the stars, the seas and indeed all the cosmos for what it is – an expression of the grace, beauty, glory and love of God. However, we should not make the mistake of believing that the choice is between a sacramental or a sacrament free, secular life. Sacramentality is built into our very being. It is the most profound part of our human nature and we can not escape it. No, the choice is rather which sacramental life do we wish to live. The sacraments of the Christian Church, where life and the whole of creation are full of grace and meaning, or the hedonism and consumerism which are the desperate and despairing sacraments of reductionism and secularism. The Christian sacraments, incorporating and presenting the incarnation of Christ, are a proclamation of hope and joy in a world full of pain and despair.

'Into the midst of darkness gathering in a world weighed down by the burden of sin and suffering is borne a faint yet unmistakable whisper, a call to the wedding

---

feast of the Apocalyptic Lamb. And the parched and cracked lips of all creation cry: 'Come Lord Jesus!'[22]

---

22   Evgeny Lampert, *The Divine Realm: Towards a theology of the Sacraments*, London: 1943, Faber and Faber Ltd, p139.

The Mystery of the Church

Every club or human institution, be it a sporting club, a university, an army or a sewing circle, has some procedures by which one becomes a member. Likewise, every human institution has rituals by which it confirms and maintains both the belonging of its members and its own identity. These procedures and rituals may be formal or informal, explicit or implicit, commented on or unnoticed, but they will exist. The type of procedure and ritual is related to the type of organization. No one would expect the local sewing circle to use the initiation rites of the local football club. So, when we consider the entry procedures and rituals for the Christian Church, the sacraments or sacred mysteries, we will need to understand the nature of the Church as it is understood by its members, since it is this understanding that will determine the way in which these sacraments are practiced and celebrated in particular Churches. Where there is a distinct difference in understanding about the nature of the Church, as there is between the Byzantine and Western Churches, this will produce distinctly different sacramental approaches – even if the difference in understanding is only a difference in emphasis. Given this, in order to understand the Byzantine Church's approach to the sacraments, we must first study the Byzantine Church's understanding of itself.

To outside commentators it is easiest to see the Church, both eastern and western, only as an institution, since the institutional elements can be seen, measured, studied and judged in secular and everyday terms. It is this face of the Church which is most like other human organisations. Yet neither the Eastern nor Western Church would regard this as an adequate understanding of the true nature of the Church. The western theologian, Avery Dulles, proposed five different models of the Church[23]. The five models proposed by Dulles fall into two distinct categories. The first category, the Church as mystical union and the Church as institution, contains those models which concern what the Church is: its nature. The second category, the Church as sacrament, as herald, and as servant, contains those models which are concerned with what the Church does: its role in the world. While the Byzantine Church would accept that each of these models is a valid aspect of the Church, they would consider that neither singly nor together do they provide a complete understanding of the nature of the Church[24]. Consider the following description of the Church by LeGuillou:

"The Church is the consummation of the creation and in her the mystery hidden in God is truly manifested. 'Chosen out before the foundation of the world', she was destined before time was to exist for all time. She was created before all else, the world was made for her, she is the 'perfect dove', the 'one home', she is the world re-made that it may be deified through the imparting of the Sprit. The Church is

---

23   Dulles, A. 1974. *Models of the Church* Doubleday and Company, New York.
24   To be fair, this is view that Dulles himself would agree with.

of Heaven, she is Heaven, as St John Chrysostom says. She is the spiritual eve, "named before the sun', the promise of the good things that the Lord has prepared. She is in truth the new creation in the Spirit. "[25]

This view of the Church is very ancient and appears in the *The Shepherd* by Hermas, a visionary work of the second century:

A maiden met me adorned like a bride from her wedding, all in white, her head veiled and wimpled; but her hair was white. Because of my former visions I recognized that she was the Church[26].

St John Chrysostom speaks of the Church being born from Christ's side at the crucifixion. Water and blood flowed from the side of Christ after he was pierced by the lance and these are considered to be symbols of Baptism and the Eucharist. Just as Eve was born from the side of Adam as he slept, so the Church is born from the side of Christ as he slept in death. Just as Eve was hailed as the spouse of Adam when he woke, so the Church is the spouse of the risen Christ. This is nothing at all like an institution of merely human organization and contrivence.

"I said that baptism and the mysteries were symbolized in that blood and water. It is from these two that the holy Church has been born 'by the washing of regeneration and the renewal of the Holy Spirit', by Baptism and the Mysteries. Now the symbols of Baptism and the Mysteries came from His side. It was from His side then that Christ formed the Church, as from the side of Adam he formed Eve. That is why in his account of the first man Moses has the words, 'bone of my bone and flesh of my flesh', giving us a hint here of the Master's side. For as at that time God took a rib from Adam's side and formed woman, so Christ gave us blood and water from His side and formed the Church. Just as then he took a rib while Adam was in a deep sleep, so now he gave the blood and water after his death. Have you seen how Christ has united his bride to himself? "[27]

The essence of the Church is that of a new (and yet ancient) spiritual creation, not a human organization. It is the body of Christ animated by the Spirit, the community of people who belong to the Lord, the spotless spouse of Christ, the fullness of creation and salvation - she is all this and more. No humanly conceived organization could mediate the Divine Grace, could impart the Spirit of God, could express the mystery of the Incarnation. These are all divine mysteries and the Church is, of her nature, so intimately connected with these mysteries that she herself is best understood as mystery. When we enter into the Church we first and foremost enter into the mystery of God.

---

25   Le Guillou, M.J. The Tradition of Eastern Orthodoxy, (London: Burns Oates, 1962) 26-27.
26   Hermas, *The Shepherd*, Vision Four.
27   St. John Chrysostom, Instructions to Catecumens.

The mystery of the Church should not be considered as something which is simply unknown (like the meaning of mystery as found in a detective novel) but as something which, even though we may know parts of it and have some partial understanding, is in its fullness unknowable – beyond the powers of the human mind to grasp. This does not downplay the role of human knowledge and understanding, but simply recognises its limitations. The mysteries of God which escape our minds are not, however, fully hidden from us. What our minds cannot grasp is revealed to us through faith and love. As Bishop Kallistos Ware says:

"In the proper religious sense of the term, 'mystery' signifies not only hiddenness but disclosure. The greek noun 'mysterion' is linked with the verb 'myein' meaning to 'close the eyes or mouth' The candidate for initiation into certain pagan mystery religions was first blindfolded and then led through a maze of passages; then suddenly his eyes were uncovered and he saw, displayed all around him, the secret emblems of the cult. So in the Christian context, we do not mean by 'mystery' merely that which is baffling and mysterious, an enigma or insoluble problem. A mystery is, on the contrary, something that is revealed for our understanding, but which we can never understand exhaustively *because it leads into the depth or the darkness of God. The eyes are closed – but they are also opened."[28]*

To appreciate the nature of this mystery we must enter into the Church's own ways of self understanding. In the Latin Church this understanding would be explicit and would be accessed mainly through a study of official Church documents such as the Dogmatic Constitution of the Church from Vatican II. The Byzantine Church, however, while it may agree with the content and sentiments of such documents, is much less analytical and more poetic and primarily finds its self-understanding in the liturgy and in the great feasts of the Church's year. The festal icons of the major feasts, in particular, express the mystery of the Church in image form. It is these two sources, the Liturgy and the Festal Icons, which can be used as a key to the self understanding of the Byzantine Church.

Rather like the Church Fathers, the Byzantine Church has never developed a systematic approach to the doctrine of the Church, while the Latin Church, likewise, has only formulated its thinking in modern times. However, the Church is a lived mystery which is very much at the centre of their faith. This is well expressed by Fr. Florovsky;

The Church gives us not a system, but a key; not a plan of God's city, but the means of entering it. Perhaps someone will lose his way because he has no plan. But all that he will see, he will see without a mediator, he will see it directly, it will be real for him; while he who has studies only the plan risks remaining outside and not really finding anything."[29]

28   Ware, K. 1995, *The Orthodox Way*, St. Vladimir's seminary Press, New York, P15.
29   Florovsky, G. 1972. The Catholicity of the Church, in *Bible, Church, Tradition: An Eastern Orthodox View* (Collected Works, Vol.1: Nordland, Mass.), P50-51. – Of course, ideally you would have both a key *and* a map.

The key turning point in human history, indeed in the history of the universe, is the entry of the Word of God, the only begotten Son of the Father, into our physical world and human existence as the child Jesus born of the Virgin Mary. The Incarnation is the central mystery of Christian belief and the Church exists to proclaim and to make manifest and present this mystery. As Timothy Ware writes in his book *The Orthodox Church:*

Between Christ and the Church there is the closest possible bond: in the famous phrase of Ignatius, 'where Christ is, there is the Catholic Church'. The Church is the extension of the incarnation, the place where the Incarnation perpetuates itself. The Church, the Greek theologian Chrestos Androutsos has written, is 'the centre and organ of Christ's redeeming work;......it is nothing else than the continuation and extension of His prophetic, priestly, and kingly power......The Church and its Founder are inextricably bound together......The Church is 'Christ with us' Christ did not leave the Church when He ascended into heaven...[30]

This understanding of the Church is expressed graphically in the Icon of the Ascension. Towards the top of the Icon, the central figure is the ascended Christ seated in a mandorla of the glory of heaven and surrounded by angels. Below Him are the apostles gathered around Mary and gazing up at Christ. The close and continuing connection between the ascended Christ and His followers is clearly evident in the geometry of the Icon. The figures of the Apostles and Mary are significantly larger than that of Christ indicating that it is now the Church which shows Christ to the world. It is in the mystery of the Church that the mystery of the Incarnation is expressed.

Hail, O Queen, glory of virgins and mothers: for your praise is beyond the eloquence of the most cultured tongues, and the wonderful manner in which you gave birth to Christ throws every intelligence into amazement. Wherefore we the faithful magnify you with one accord.

Hirmos, Pentecost.

Central to the icon of the Ascension is the figure of Mary. If this is an icon of the Church, then this suggests that Mary is central to the Church. It is noticeable that Mary is centrally placed and that she is looking outwards to the viewer rather than towards Christ. Christ also looks out at the viewer and the connection between Mary and Christ, who is directly above her, is particularly strong. In the Byzantine Church Mary is not primarily a model of Christian living to be emulated and loved, but is regarded with awe because of her role in the mystery of the Incarnation and the story of salvation. As Nicholas Cabasilas said:

The Incarnation was not only the work of the Father, of His Power and His

---

30   Ware, T. 1963, *The Orthodox Church*, Penguin Books, Middelsex, P245.

Traditional Festal Icon of the Ascension

Spirit......but it was also the work of the will and faith of the Virgin.......Just as God became incarnate voluntarily, so He wished that His Mother should bear Him freely and with her full consent[31].

Mary is always the Theotokos, the Mother of God, and she is also therefore the Mother of the Church – Christ's mystical body. She is also, however, a member of the Church and is the image of the glorified Church which brings Christ to the world.

You faithful ones, let us hymn the crown of the universe, Heaven's gateway, Mary the Virgin, flower of the human race and forth-bringer of God. She is the home and temple of the Godhead, she overturned sin's landmarks, she is the confirmation of

---

31   Cabasilas, C. 1926, *On the Annunciation*, 4-5, in *Patrologia Orientalis*, Vol XIX, Paris, P488.

our faith. The Lord born of her is fighting for us. Go forward boldly, you people of God, for he, the all-mighty has vanquished the foe.

Dogmatikon, Oktoekhos.

In both the Eastern and Western Church the great feast of Pentecost is pivotal for understanding the nature of the Church. The very earliest iconographic representation of Pentecost, the Rabbala Codex of 586 AD, also gives artistic and theological prominence to Mary as image of the Church. It looks forward to the later theology of the Palamite school, which hailed Mary as the 'Spirit-bearer' in the Church between the time of the lord's Ascension and the event of Pentecost. This accords with accounts in scripture and has been retained in the Western Church's portrayal of Pentecost. In later portrayals, Mary is, however, absent from the traditional Byzantine icon of Pentecost.

The traditional Byzantine Icon of Pentecost shows the Apostles sitting in a semi-circle with the flames of the Spirit above their heads. Above them, at the top of the icon, an arc of gold and black shows the glory and mystery of heaven, while at their feet there is darkness. In this darkness there is the figure of an old man dressed in a king's robes and carrying a scroll. This figure is "Old Man Cosmos" who represents all of creation. He is in darkness because creation has fallen into sin and decay. This Icon clearly expresses one aspect of the Church. It is the community of people filled with the Spirit who sit between the decay of the world and the glory of heaven. It is this Spirit-filled community, gathered around the apostles – their bishops, who can act as a bridge and bring about the salvation of the Cosmos. The key point here is the presence of the Spirit. It is not through human eloquence or wisdom that the Church can bring about the salvation of the world, but only by being the bearer of the Spirit to the world. This point is emphasised in the liturgy of the feast.

Blessed are you, Christ our God, who have filled the fishermen with wisdom by sending down the Holy Spirit upon them and who, through them, have united the world. Glory to You, O Lover of Mankind!

Troparion from the Holy and Glorious Pentecost Sunday

The Holy Spirit provides every gift: He inspires prophecy, perfects the priesthood, grants wisdom to the illiterate, makes simple fishermen to become wise theologians, and establishes perfect order in the organization of the Church. Wherefore, O Comforter, equal in nature and majesty with the Father and the Son, Glory to You!

Portion of the Stichera of Pentecost

Filled and sanctified by the Spirit so as to do the will of the Father and bring Christ to the world, the Church is caught up in the life of the Trinity: in the very life of

God. It is this life which its own life of prayer and liturgy expresses. The Church therefore is a sacrament of the Trinity, continually expressing the very life of the Godhead in the heart of creation and thereby raising creation to that life which is its destiny: to be one with God. This process of divinization may be invisible, but it is also inexorable. Even the sin of its members cannot effect the essential nature and destiny of the Church since together the sinners who make up the Church become something different from what they are as individuals: through the power and grace of the Spirit they become the body of Christ.

The Church therefore looks forward to the end times, to the final and full realisation of the Kingdom of God. However, the Church also anticipates this realization of the kingdom. It is a taste of the life of heaven even here on Earth. As Khomiakov says; *The Church, even on Earth, is a thing of heaven.* Timothy Ware writes; *It* (the

Traditional Festal Icon of the Feast of Pentecost

Church) *stands at a point of intersection between the Present Age and the Age to Come, and it lives in both Ages at once[32].*

Here also Mary is a crucial figure in the Church's understanding of itself. As Lossky writes:

......the very heart of the Church, one of her most secret mysteries, her mystical centre, her perfection already realized in a human person fully united with God, finding herself beyond the resurrection and judgment. This person is Mary, the Mother of God. She who gave human nature to the Word and brought forth God become man, gave herself freely to become the instrument of the incarnation which was brought to pass in her nature purified by the Holy Spirit. But the Holy Spirit descended once more upon the Virgin, on the day of Pentecost; not this time to avail Himself of her nature as an instrument, but to give Himself to her, to become the means of her deification. So the most pure nature which itself contained the Word, entered into perfect union with the deity in the person of the Mother of God.[33]

It is from this understanding of the Church that the Byzantine Church develops its understanding of the role of beauty in worship. If the Church is a creature of heaven, then this should be evident in its liturgy and even in the buildings. Entering a Byzantine Church, the believer is surrounded by a crowd of saints (in their icons) and led towards God in the sanctuary. The beauty of the liturgy, the beauty of the Church building with its icons, even the smell of the incense, all combine to form a powerful symbol of heaven – a heaven already, though imperfectly, present.

The icons which fill the Church serve as a point of meeting between heaven and earth. As each local congregation prays Sunday by Sunday, surrounded by the figures of Christ, the angels, and the saints, these visible images remind the faithful unceasingly of the invisible presence of the whole company of heaven at the Liturgy. The faithful can feel the walls of the Church open out upon eternity, and they are helped to realize that their Liturgy on earth is one and the same with the great Liturgy of heaven[34].

---

32   Ware, *The Orthodox Church*, Penguin Books, Middelsex
33   Lossky, V. *The Mystical Theology of the Eastern Church*, St. Valdimir's Seminary Press, Crestwood, N.Y, .p.193
34   Ware, *The Orthodox Church*, Penguin Books, Middelsex., P277

Sacramental Theology

Christianity is not a highly refined "spiritual" religion. It has a persistent connection with the ash and the dust of this world. Christian life is not a Manichean struggle where the good spirit battles against the evil flesh. No, for the Christian, all creation is sacred both because of its creation by God and because it is caught up in the paschal mystery of Christ's death and resurrection.

"for creation waits with eager longing for the revealing of the sons of God; for creation was subjected to futility, not of its own will but by the will of him who subjected it in hope; because the creation itself will be set free from its bondage to decay and obtain the glorious liberty of the children of God." Rom 8: 19-21.

The Incarnation has changed forever the spiritual state not just of Christians, nor just of humans, but of all creation. The physical world then, including our bodies, is not a barrier to the grace of God but rather a vehicle for it. This is why the Church has sacraments. They are visible signs, using the materials of the physical world, of God's invisible grace.

The Church, both east and west, believes that the sacraments were instituted, at least implicitly, by Christ. Yet for nearly a thousand years the seven sacraments as we now know them, were not closely defined. The Church knew that there were sacraments and that there were many other actions which were in some way similar to them in nature. The precise number and character of the sacraments was left to the mystery of Christ's action in his Church. Eventually the seven great sacraments of the Church became defined around the great events and constant realities of normal human life – birth, growth, food, work marriage, sickness and death. Characteristically, this definition of the seven great sacraments happened first in the Western Church and was picked up later by the Eastern Church who were less concerned with definition and placed greater emphasis on the general sacramental character of Christian life.

However, neither in the East nor the West is the ritual life of the Church limited to these seven great sacraments alone. Rather, this life extends through a variety of actions to bring the grace of God to every facet of human life (eg. blessing a house, blessing a fishing fleet and even blessing pets and other animals) and so make it sacred. Sacraments, in their broadest sense, link the Church to the community and make the stuff of the everyday lives of the people of God sacred.

Mystery (mysterion) is the word used for sacrament in the Byzantine Church. *Sacrament,* on the other hand, as a word comes from the Latin word *sacramentum* and it relates to a legal sign or dedication. It is a word for a legal contract which goes beyond mere legal application to include the personal honor of the individual. An example was the *sacramentum militia* which was the oath taken by a Roman legionary as he joined the army and paraded past the legion's eagle standard as a sign of their loyalty. The Roman *sacramentum* means that you dedicate yourself and receive dedication in return. The Latin Church adapted the term and in religious terms it is a sign of the covenant between God and His Church. The Church's sacraments are then at the core of God's relationship with His people.

The Byzantine Church has never used this term, which has a quasi-legal resonance. Rather, it uses the term *mysterion*, or mystery. The term *mysterion* referred to something that was only revealed to those who had been initiated. As was noted earlier; *"..in the Christian context, we do not mean by 'mystery' merely that which is baffling and mysterious, an enigma or insoluble problem. A mystery is, on the contrary, something that is revealed for our understanding, but which we can never understand exhaustively because it leads into the depth or the darkness of God."*[35]

In Church usage there are two senses in which the revelation of these mysteries occurs. The first is the revelation of God in the person of Christ Jesus which can only be known by the initiation of faith (the mystery of the Incarnation) and the second is the symbolic but real participation in the life of the Word of God made man made possible through the faithful celebration of His Church. This revelation is only possible to the person of faith. An unbeliever may have well have academic knowledge about the mystery, but the core of the mystery will always escape them. Thus St. John Chrysostom writes of the Eucharist:

It is called a mystery because what we believe is not the same as what we see, but we see one thing and believe another…….When I hear the Body of Christ mentioned, I understand what is said in one sense, the unbeliever in another[36].

It is important here to make a clear distinction between the concept of a symbol and a sign. Even though these terms are often used interchangeably in common speech, and particularly in the language and terminology of modern technology, they (the sign and the symbol) have very different relationships to the underlying reality they point to. A sign is an arbitrary label which is determined by a particular human culture and may not make any sense at all to anyone not from that culture. For example, the number 60 inside a red circle has no relationship to speed or law, and a large yellow "M" has no relationship to cheap food, apart from the arbitrary human decisions to assign these meanings. A symbol on the other hand is connected to what it symbolises by its own nature. Thus a candle can be a symbol of the light of Christ because it gives light, water can be a symbol of new life and blessing because it literally gives life. A symbol has an ontological connection with

---

35   Ware, K. 1995, *The Orthodox Way*, St. Vladimir's seminary Press, New York, P15.
36   Chrysostom, J. *Homilies on 1 Corinthians*, 711

what it symbolises not just an arbitrary connection assigned by human culture.

It follows from this that if a symbol is to be used liturgically, then it must be used in a way which allows its nature to show forth: water must flow, oil must ooze. If the nature of the symbol is not evident then it will cease to function as a symbol. It will become a mechanical action and, at best, be only a sign of the sacred reality. It will loose its capacity to act as a true meeting place between the transcendent God and the physical world which is His creation. As Evgeny Lampert says:

It is essential for the understanding of the symbol to be aware of its fundamentally two-sided, two-edged nature: in it there takes place a living meeting of a transcendent and an immanent reality – not in the abstract philosophical, but in the concrete religious meaning of these terms. .....The symbol is thus a truly divine-human reality in which both God and creature are operative. Apart from this it turns into a mere convention or else remains a bare and dead empirical object devoid of any meaning[37].

There is a great tendency in our modern society to reduce symbols to mere signs. This stems from a secular view of the world which views the universe not as the Spirit filled creation but as a cold, external and empty void, devoid of human meaning and independent of and indifferent to human existence. In such a view of the universe a symbol, in the sense that we have been discussing it, is impossible since there is no ultimate meaning to connect to – to symbolise. At best a symbol is a sign of a humanly derived and determined meaning. This is not the traditional Christian view of the world and most specifically, not the view of the Byzantine Church. The Byzantine Church has a symbolic understanding of the world where everything is seen as a symbol of the action of God in the world and where the very existence of the universe is wholly dependent on, indeed is a function of, its relationship to God. Again from Evgeny Lampert:

The symbolic interpretation of the world, according to which all things visible are a symbol of the invisible, and all things material are a symbol of the spirit, is a witness to just this transcendent-immanent significance nature of the symbol; it is a witness of the transcendent meaning of all things, and of the presence of the Holy Spirit in them, His 'meeting' and utter union with the life of the world and man[38].

There is another way in which modern society approaches the physical world and that is the pantheistic, magical view of the various New Age cults, many of whom misconstrue and misappropriate the spiritual traditions of indigenous cultures. Here nature is seen as having meaning but it not a symbolic meaning which points to the transcendent God, rather it is a human meaning which inevitably points back to the human person and the "Gods" come to have all the failings of the humans

---

37   Lampert, E. 1943, *The Divine Realm* Faber and Faber Ltd., London, P112.
38   ibid, P111

who approach them. It was this pagan view of the sacred that the Hebrews rejected when they condemned graven images. This is a profoundly unsatisfactory view of the world since:

The life of nature is double-faced and the veil of light may conceal nocturnal darkness. Nature knows her chasms and horrors. She followed man in his fall and has since remained in a state of frustration and disintegration. She is orphaned without man who has fallen away from her, because he fell away from God; she has become the dwelling place of earthly-demons. Despite her real symbolic power she is in need of transfiguration; she is not a self-contained and self-completed "circle'...

If creation is so fallen, then how can it act as a symbol of, indeed as a vehicle for God's grace?   Lampert's reply is given in his final passage:

'Into the midst of darkness gathering in a world weighed down by the burden of sin and suffering is borne a faint yet unmistakable whisper, a call to the wedding feast of the Apocalyptic Lamb. And the parched and cracked lips of all creation cry: 'Come Lord Jesus!'"[39]

One part of the answer is that although the image of God was disfigured in the fall, it was never erased, neither in creation or in man, but the fullness of the answer lies in the mystery of the incarnation.

With the coming of the God-man and Saviour Jesus Christ, with his death on Golgotha there took place a shattering and mighty exorcism of the cosmos and Nature from within: 'Great Pan has died', the demonic possession of Nature is forthwith broken, the Prince of this world is driven out, and Nature awaits her final transformation in the eschatological fulfillment.....Christ could not have fulfilled his cosmic exorcism, if Nature were not herself an ever-living witness to the Holy Spirit, whereby she cries in man and through man: Abba, Father!'[40]

When Christ became man He transformed the stuff of this world into His own divinity. As the fathers of the Church proclaimed; he became man so that we might become God. Nor is it just the human race that is transformed by the Word of God taking material form, St Paul writes of all creation waiting in joy for the glorious liberty of the sons of God. All creation is transformed by the incarnation. It is returned to its true nature and made, as it was always meant to be, into a vehicle for God's grace and life. The life of Christ reveals the sacramental nature of all creation and its true nature and destiny.

---

39   Ibid.
40   *Divine Realm*, 116.

As John Forest writes when discussing the icon of Jesus' baptism:

Just as the Son of God became a man of flesh and blood through Mary, he used the material things of our world as means of salvation: water, wine, oil and bread. The water we bath in, the water we drink - the water that is the main component of our bodies – every drop of water connects us with the water in which Jesus was baptized. In Jesus' baptism all water has forever been blessed.[41]

All of creation is not only blessed in the incarnation but it regains its original destiny. At the end times, together with the Church, all creation will be brought to the Father by the Son through the power of the Spirit and will be adopted into the very life of the Trinity as the mystical body of Christ embraces all things. Creation is transformed, divinized and brought to the full communion for which it was always intended. This is why in the sacramental life of the Church water can bring the life of the Spirit, bread can become the Body of Christ, wine can become His Blood. In its sacramental life, the Church not only brings all the people before God but all of creation as well and there transforms them by the power of the Spirit so that the dust and ash of this world are made holy and filled with divine glory. This is the process known in the Byzantine Church as 'theosis' and it is a hallmark of the Byzantine Churches' sacramental theology.

As Lampert writes:

'while sacraments and their power arise within the human and cosmic world of un-transfigured nature, they transcend the limits of this age and reach out to the world to come. That ray of transfiguration, that light of Mount Tabor, is not extinguished, but shines mysteriously in Christ's sacraments; and all creation seeks and longs for it. The sacrament, while it arises and is realized within this world, also reaches out to the beyond. It is a prophecy and anticipation, and thence the realization of God as 'all in all', in whom the whole cosmos is destined to become a sacrament, and man's creative, divine-human calling to be fulfilled..'[42]

All of this may sound strange to the ears of Latin Christians who are more used to the mutual dedication of the *sacramentum* model. A very fine expression of this concept, however, comes from an unlikely source. The following passage was written by a young scientist who was also a Jesuit and a priest and a product of the French branch of the Latin Church. He was conscripted into the French army and found himself in the trenches of WWI without any of the means to fulfill his priestly office. That he could write the following passage is a sign of hope that the Churches, East and West, may not be as far apart as either fear.

Since today Lord, I your priest have neither bread, nor wine, nor altar, I shall

41   Forest, Jim Praying With Icons, Maryknoll New York: Orbis Books, 2002.
42   Divine Realm, 139.

spread my hands over the whole universe and take its immensity as the matter of my
sacrifice. Is not the infinite circle of things the one final Host that it is your will to
transmute ... ... Take up in your hands, Lord, and bless this universe that is destined
to sustain and fulfill the plenitude of your being amongst us. Make this universe
ready to be united with you: and that this may be so, intensify the magnetism that
comes down from your heart to draw to it the dust of which we are made[43].

It should be clear by now that a proper sacramental understanding requires a
radically different world view from the rational, reductionist view of the secular
humanist. It is a world view that sees transcendent significance in the things of
nature and knows the Sprit to act powerfully in the lives of Christians. You do
not just wake up with this new world view one day, nor is it something you can
learn in a course. This world view requires a new life, a life filled with the Spirit
of God, which only God can give. You have to be born into this new life through
the sacraments of initiation; Baptism, Chrismation (confirmation) and Eucharist.
While there are seven sacraments officially listed by the Church, both east and
west, not all of these sacraments are considered to be of the same importance.
The Church has always recognised the central importance of the sacraments of
initiation, Baptism, Chrismation (confirmation) and Eucharist, in the life of the
Christian. This is not so say that the others are unimportant but rather that these
three form the core of Christian life.

In the early Church, the catechumens (those who desired to become Christians),
at the end of their period of instruction, would be brought to the Church by their
sponsor (normally a friend who knew them well and could vouch for them to the
community) without being told why. In times of persecution this would often be
done at night and in secret. They would be taken to the baptistery, stripped and
fully immersed three times in a baptismal font which resembled a tomb, as the
Trinitarian formula was pronounced over them – *I baptise you in the name of*
the Father and of the Son and of the Holy Spirit. The genders were, of course,
separated to preserve propriety and deaconesses saw to the needs of the women,
although a priest would have done the actual baptising. As they stepped from the
tomb-like font, they would be clothed in a white garment to symbolise the new life
they had embraced. They would then be presented to the bishop who would anoint
them with oil and lay his hands on them to initiate them into full membership of the
Church. Finally they would be taken to the celebration of the Eucharist where they
would take communion for the first time. It was only after this that the significance
of the actions would be explained. The symbolic understanding would come first
and the rational understanding would follow.

The Byzantine Church has retained the unity of these sacraments. Baptism,

---

43   Teilhard de Chardin, *Writings in Time of War,* as quoted in Sproxton V. *Teilhard de Chardin* SCM Press,
       London, 1971, p47.

Chrismation and first Eucharist all take place together as the one act of Christian initiation. In the Latin West, more by a set of historical circumstances than by conscious decision, these sacraments became separated with Confirmation and First Eucharist happening many years after Baptism. Indeed, the order of the sacraments was altered so that children would receive their first Eucharist before their Confirmation. This was recognised as a problem during the Second Vatican Council which re-established the unity and proper order of these sacraments for adults in the Rite of Christian Initiation of Adults (RCIA). Many Latin Dioceses have also sought to do this for children by celebrating Confirmation and first Eucharist together.

The Byzantine Church has always insisted on the unity of these sacraments and while we will subsequently treat each of them separately, it should be remembered that in the Byzantine Church they are closely connected. Indeed, they all form part of the one event – the bringing to life of a new creature in Christ; a child of God who, as a priest, can gather all the praises of the universe and present them to God.

Baptism - To Put On Christ

When St John Chrysostom gave his first instruction to the catecumens, he first welcomed them as proto-members of the community, anticipating their initiation. Membership of the believing community is thus a primary outcome of the forthcoming sacramental initiation. He later expressed the powerful connection between Baptism and salvation through incorporation into the believing community which is the image of the crucified Christ giving His substance to His Church, His mystical spouse.

"The gospel relates that when Christ had died and was still hanging on the cross, the soldier approached him and pierced His side with the spear, and at once there came out water and blood. The one was the symbol of baptism and the other of the mysteries.....I said that baptism and the mysteries were symbolized in that blood and water......Now the symbols of Baptism and the Mysteries came from His side. It was from His side then that Christ formed the Church, as from the side of Adam he formed Eve........For as at that time God took a rib from Adam's side and formed woman, so Christ gave us blood and water from His side and formed the Church. Just as then he took a rib while Adam was in a deep sleep, so now he gave the blood and water after his death. Have you seen how Christ has united his bride to himself?"[44]

Christians are not saved as individuals, but as members of the Church of God which forms His Kingdom, His spouse, His bride. The catechumens are thus about to enter this kingdom, to join in the nuptial celebrations. At the end of his introductory welcome, St John writes:

"Remember me, therefore, when you come into that kingdom, when you receive the royal robe, when you are girt with the purple dipped in the master's blood, when you will be crowned with the diadem, which has lustre leaping forth from it on all sides, more brilliant than the rays of the sun. Such are the gifts of the Bridegroom, greater indeed than your worth, but worthy of his loving kindness[45]."

This is clearly no mere entry into a community nor simply a moral renunciation and dedication, although this is indeed part of the mystery. Rather, something momentous and strange is about to take place in the lives of these catechumens. After this they will not be as they were before, but will have entered into a new life which can only be described in terms of ecstatic metaphor which they can not yet fully understand.

---

44   St. John Chrysostom, Instructions to Catecumens. CAT3
45   ibid

Later in the same discourse he describes the nature of Baptism by reflecting on all the different names that have been applied to it.

"But, if you will, let us discourse about the name which this mystic cleansing bears: for its name is not one, but very many and various. For this purification is called the laver of regeneration. "He saved us," he saith, "through the laver of regeneration, and renewing of the Holy Ghost." It is called also illumination, and this St. Paul again has called it, "For call to remembrance the former days in which after ye were illuminated ye endured a great conflict of sufferings;" and again, "For it is impossible for those who were once illuminated, and have tasted of the heavenly gift, and then fell away, to renew them again unto repentance." It is called also, baptism: "For as many of you as were baptized into Christ did put on Christ." It is called also burial: "For we were buried" saith he, "with him, through baptism, into death." It is called circumcision: "In whom ye were also circumcised, with a circumcision not made with hands, in the putting off of the body of the sins of the flesh." It is called a cross: "Our old man was crucified with him that the body of sin might be done away.[46]"

In Jewish law circumcision is a sign of the covenant between God and His people. A child, or man, who is circumcised becomes one of the people of Israel, the chosen people. He is claimed for God. This sense of someone being chosen and claimed for God carries over into Christian Baptism. At the very beginning of the ceremony the candidate is asked if they reject Satan. In saying yes, the candidate is turning away from their old life and beliefs and dedicating themselves to God. A prayer of exorcism is then said to drive out any influence of the devil which may have settled in the soul as a result of past pagan life.

In the twenty first century we are very wary of things such as demons and exorcism and tend to attribute evil to psychological causes. However, it is Christian doctrine, in both the Latin and Byzantine Churches, that there is a personal force for evil external to man who influences human affairs to cause suffering and sin – to destroy the human race. In the society of the pagan Roman Empire this was considered self-evident. It was seen to be manifest in the apparently effective parapsychological phenomena that were prominent in pagan society – fortune telling, good luck charms, curses and the like.

While the Christian community seems to have been more sceptical of these magical powers than most of the society, they did not doubt the presence and action of evil. The prayer of exorcism was seen as very necessary. In our current, post-Christian society, where superstition has replaced religion and where book shops are crowded with books on neo-paganism, fortune telling, spirit guides, mediums and other New Age paraphernalia, we may need to recover a sense of the reality and influence of

---

46   ibid

evil and come to see the prayer of exorcism, not as a quaint hangover from another time, but as a real and pressing necessity.

After the prayer of exorcism the candidate enters the baptismal font for the 'mystical washing' of baptism. In the Byzantine Church this is, literally a true bath, which has strong connections to the everyday washing away of the dirt and grime of our normal lives. Here the symbolism is clear. This is a real washing, a mystical washing, which will wash the candidate clean at a very deep level.

The symbolism of being immersed in water, however, goes much further than simple cleaning. It calls to mind significant events in the story of salvation such as; Noah's Ark where the old sinful world was drowned and a new world born; the passage trough the Red Sea where the chains of sinful Egypt were destroyed and God's people celebrated His glory and power; the passage across the River Jordan where the years of being lost and wandering in the desert were over and the people entered the land of God's promise, and the ritual washing of the Jewish law which could remove the religious uncleanliness of the body. As St. John Chrysostom says:

"You did not see Pharaoh drowned with his armies, but you have seen the devil with his weapons overcome by the waters of baptism. The Israelites passed through the sea; you have passed from death to life. They were delivered from the Egyptians; you have been delivered from the powers of darkness. The Israelites were freed from slavery to a pagan people; you have been freed from the much greater slavery to sin."[47]

Finally, Christian baptism is linked to the baptism of the Forerunner, John the Baptist, who with trembling hands baptised the Word of God Incarnate. Baptism is a very special kind of ritual washing. In Christian thought it stems from the actions of John the Baptist, although there are older precedents, both Jewish and pagan. The baptism of John went much deeper than the normal ritual washing of Jewish custom. It was a call to repentance, a washing away of sins from those of "humbled and contrite" heart. In this it was a prototype, an anticipation of Christian baptism, which is far deeper and whose consequences lead not just to the forgiveness of sin, but to the complete regeneration of the person. *"I baptise you with water but He will baptise you with the Holy Spirit and with fire."*

While Baptism does remove all sin and traces of sin from the newly Christian soul, this is only the beginning. A new creature is being "born of water and the Holy Spirit", a new child of God who will grow into the glory of divinity, a new priest who will offer up a sacrifice of praise for all creation.

In order for this to happen, of course, the old person must die and be resurrected. This connection between the cross and baptism was spelt out by St. John Chrysostom in

---

47   ibid

a later catecetical instruction:

"The gospel relates that when Christ had died and was still hanging on the cross, the soldier approached him and pierced His side with the spear, and at once there came out water and blood. The one was the symbol of baptism and the other of the mysteries. That soldier, then, pierced his side, he breached the wall of the holy temple and found the treasure and acquired the wealth."[48]

So Christian baptism is a consequence of the crucifixion. We are not baptised in the Red Sea or the River Jordon. We are baptised in the water flowing from the side of the crucified Christ. And because baptism allows us to share in His Crucifixion, it also allows us to share in His Resurrection. This image of baptism as a dying, a sharing in the cross and burial of Christ, is strongly expressed in the Byzantine baptismal rite. The old person dies in the waters of baptism by sharing in the death of Christ on the cross so that as they rise from the water they are rising with Christ to new life. This is why many of the old baptismal fonts resembled coffins or tombs. The symbolism was that you enter the tomb (death) as the old person and rise from the waters of baptism to a new life in Christ as a new child of God. This is best expressed in symbolic terms by full immersion. The normal practice in the Latin Church of Baptism by the pouring of water, which in the Byzantine Church is only used as an emergency measure, does not convey this same symbolism of dying and rising. For this reason, many parishes within the Latin Church are now trying to re-establish full immersion as the normal mode of baptism.

The "resurrection" of the person in Baptism also has the sense of returning to a primal goodness, of undoing all the harm and corruption of the soul caused by sin. This is the regeneration spoken of by St. John Chrysostom. By washing the soul clean of all traces of sin, Baptism "regenerates" the Christian as God wishes them to be. The effects of the fall (original Sin) are done away with and the new Christian stands innocent before God.

For this reason the new Christian is clothed in a new white garment in order to symbolise their purity at the start of their new life in Christ. The white of the new robe is not only a symbol of purity. It is also a symbol of light. The new Christian has come from the dark of their old life into the light of Christ.

"The Israelites could not look on the face of Moses in glory, though he was their fellow servant and kinsman. But you have seen the face of Christ in his glory."[49]

This is why one of St. John Chrysostom's names for Baptism is illumination and why St. Gregory of Nazianus (see below) refers to it as enlightenment. The new Christian has been given the light and will now live in the light and truth of the

---

48   ibid
49   ibid

Christian faith which has set them free. This new life, of course, is not like the old life. It has new responsibilities and a new way of living. That is why so much of St. John Chrysostom's catechesis is taken up with moral instruction. The new Christian needed to know how to live as a Christian and how to express this new life that they had received. That the living of this new life will be hard is not hidden. It is why the next step in their initiation is the sacrament of Chrismation (Confirmation).

After being robed in white, joyfully the new Christians are brought before the bishop (in the practice of the ancient Church) as new members of the community. It is now the practice in the Byzantine Church for the sacrament of Chrismation to be administered by a priest on behalf of the bishop. The chrism, consecrated by the bishop, expresses the connection with the bishop. The practice of the bishop himself presiding at confirmation is still preserved in the Latin Church.

There is great joy at the arrival of these new Christians expressed in the ancient texts. They are referred to as new stars shining brightly in the sky. They are a sign of the life of the community. To baptise, to bring people to life in Christ, is central and necessary to the life of the Church. In his own instructions to catechumens, St. Gregory of Nazianus, called the Theologian, describes Baptism, in the following way. He calls it Enlightenment, it is:

"The splendour of souls, the conversion of life, the question put to the Godward conscience. It is the aid to our weakness, the renunciation of the flesh, the following of the Spirit, the fellowship of the Word, the improvement of the creature, the overwhelming of sin, the participation of light, the dissolution of darkness. It is the carriage to God, the dying with Christ, the perfecting of the mind, the bulwark of Faith, the key of the Kingdom of heaven, the change of life, the removal of slavery, the loosing of chains, the remodelling of the whole man. Why should I go into further detail? Enlightenment is the greatest and most magnificent of the gifts of God. For just as we speak of the Holy of Holies, and the Song of Songs, as more comprehensive and more excellent than others, so is this called Enlightenment, as being more holy than any other illumination which we possess."[50]

---

50   Gregory Nazianzus, Oration 40, The Oration on Holy Baptism.

Chrismation - Seal of the Holy Spirit

When Paul convinced the people at Ephesus to become Christian they entered into their new life as Christians through Baptism and the "laying on of hands". The two actions were performed sequentially, but they were distinct. It was only after the laying on of hands that the new Christians of Ephesus entered fully into Christian life and began to speak in tongues and to prophesy[51]. We see that from apostolic times there existed the early forms of two closely connected but distinct sacraments of initiation: baptism and the "laying on of hands". This is called Confirmation in the Latin Church or Chrismation in the Byzantine Church and another passage in Acts gives us more information about the relationship between these two sacraments.

"When the apostles in Jerusalem heard the Samarians had accepted the word of God, they sent Peter and John to them and they went down there and prayed for the Samarians to receive the Holy Spirit, for as yet he had not come down on any of them: they had only been baptised in the name of the Lord Jesus. Then they laid their hands on them and they received the Holy Spirit."[52]

A number of things are clear about Confirmation/Chrismation from this passage. First, it is a distinct rite, expressed in the laying on of hands, which was needed to complete the initiation of the Samaritan Christians. Secondly, while there was a delay between the Baptism of the Samaritans by the Deacon Phillip and their Confirmation/Chrismation, this was not seen as desirable. Peter and John set out the complete the task. However, they did not re-baptise. The validity of the Baptism by Phillip was not called into question. The third thing to note is the strong connection between this sacrament and the Apostles. The Deacon Phillip could baptise, but only the Apostles could confer Confirmation/Chrismation.

In apostolic times then, Confirmation/Chrismation was conferred by an apostle after baptism, preferably immediately after, and it brought about an indwelling of the Holy Spirit which manifested itself in charismatic gifts. This understanding of the sacrament passed into the early Church with the role of the apostle being transformed into by that of the bishop.

Baptism in the early Church was always, except in emergency situations, followed immediately by the laying on of hands by the bishop and the anointing with the special perfumed oil called chrism (or myron) which was used in the Old Testament for the consecration of priests, prophets, and kings. It is described by Tertullian writing around 200 AD.

---

51   Acts 19:5
52   Acts 8:14

"Then having gone up from the bath we are anointed with a blessed anointing of ancient discipline, by which people were accustomed to be anointed for priesthood, by oil from a horn from which Aaron was anointed by Moses [Ex 30:22-30]. For this reason we were called "christs" ("anointed ones") from "chrism," which is the ointment which lends its name to the Lord. It was made spiritual because the Lord was anointed with the Spirit by God the Father, as it says in Acts: 'For they were gathered together in that city against your holy Son whom you have anointed [Acts 4:27].' Thus also the anointing flows on us physically, but benefits spiritually, as the physical act of baptism (that we are immersed in water) has a spiritual effect (that we are free from transgressions). Next, calling and inviting the Holy Spirit, the hand is imposed for the blessing."[53]

A fuller description of the ancient sacramental procedure is given in the following extract from Hippolytus around the year 215 AD.

"The neophytes are anointed by the presbyter from the oil consecrated by the bishop. He says, 'I anoint you with holy oil in the name of Jesus Christ.' And thus, drying themselves, the individuals are vested, and afterwards are brought in the Church. But the bishop, imposing his hand on them, prays by saying, 'Lord God, who made them worthy to merit the forgiveness of sins by the bath of rebirth of the Holy Spirit, send your grace onto them, that they may serve you according to your will. For to you is the glory, to the Father and to the Son with the Holy Spirit in the Holy Church, both now and for ever. Amen.' Afterwards, pouring the consecrated oil from his hand and imposing it on the neophyte's head, let him say, 'I anoint you with holy oil in the Lord, the Father Almighty, and Christ Jesus, and the Holy Spirit.'"[54]

There are three stages mentioned here – the newly baptized are brought to the Church, the bishop lays hands on them and then anoints them with oil. In the first stage the newly baptized are presented to the bishop who is the leader and teacher of the local Church. He greets them and welcomes them to the community. Once again, Christianity is a communal religion. Christians are not Christians on their own. They are always part of the Church. The bishop then lays his hands on them. This is an ancient gesture of blessing, healing and acceptance. Here though, it also has the sense of commissioning and empowering and it is significant that the bishop's actions here are similar to his actions in ordaining a new priest or deacon. Here the new Christian is commissioned to their life as a member of God's priestly people and given the power and gifts needed to live this new life through the grace of the Holy Spirit. Living as a Christian in a pagan world is not easy and it is through the sacrament of Chrismation that the new Christian is given the strength they need to be priest, prophet and king to a lost world. They were then anointed

---

53   Tertullian, On Baptism 7-8 (c. 200 AD)
54   Hippolytus, Apostolic Tradition 21-22 (c. 215 AD)

with sacred oil which marked them as chosen and consecrated for this task. In the ancient Church then, Chrismation welcomed and confirmed the newly baptized as full members of the believing community, blessed them with the grace of the Holy Spirit needed to live their new lives as Christians and marked them as chosen by God and sacred to Him. They are sanctified, made holy, and filled with the power and the living presence of the Holy Spirit.

Both the Byzantine and Latin Churches believe that the Christian is filled with the Spirit at Confirmation and that the power and strength needed to live a Christian life is given to them. Both believe that graces (or gifts) of the Spirit are given to the Christian at confirmation. However, while the Latin Church has analyzed scripture in order to define the seven gifts of the Spirit, and their resultant fruits that are given in the sacrament, the Byzantine Church has always taken a more poetic and less prescriptive approach, preferring to leave the exact nature of the gifts given to each soul by the Spirit to the mystery and exigencies of Christian life.

Water comes down from heaven as rain, and although it is always the same in itself, it produces many different effects, one in the palm tree, another in the vine, and so on throughout the whole of creation. It does not come down, now as one thing, now as another, but while remaining essentially the same, it adapts itself to the needs of every creature that receives it. In the same way the Holy Spirit, whose nature is always the same, simple and indivisible, apportions grace to each man as he wills. Like a dry tree which puts forth shoots when watered, the soul bears the fruit of holiness when repentance has made it worthy of receiving the Holy Spirit. Although the Spirit never changes, the effects of his action, by the will of God and in the name of Christ, are both many and marvellous. The Spirit makes one man a teacher of divine truth, inspires another to prophesy, gives another the power of casting out devils, enables another to interpret Holy Scripture. The Spirit strengthens one man's self-control, shows another how to help the poor, teaches another to fast and lead a life of asceticism, makes another oblivious to the needs of the body, trains another for martyrdom. His action is different in different people, but the Spirit himself is always the same. In each person, Scripture says, the Spirit reveals his presence in a particular way for the common good. The Spirit comes gently and makes himself known by his fragrance. He is not felt as a burden, for he is light, very light. Rays of light and knowledge stream before him as he approaches. The Spirit comes with the tenderness of a true friend and protector to save, to heal, to teach, to counsel, to strengthen, to console. The Spirit comes to enlighten the mind first of the one who receives him, and then, through him, the minds of others as well[55].

Here the early Church drew a close parallel with the baptism of Jesus. After Jesus was baptized by John, the Holy Spirit descended on Him and He began His mission.

---

55   St Cyril of Jerusalem, The Holy Spirit as Living Water

This was seen as the type of Christian initiation. The catechumens when baptized, were born again in innocence, and then the Holy Spirit descended on them through the anointing with holy oil. This is clearly explained by St. Cyril of Jerusalem in his instructions to catechumens.

"Christ bathed in the river Jordan, imparting to its waters the fragrance of his divinity, and when he came up from them the Holy Spirit descended upon him, like resting upon like. So we also, after coming up from the sacred waters of baptism, were anointed with chrism, which signifies the Holy Spirit, by whom Christ was anointed.....The oil of gladness with which Christ was anointed was a spiritual oil; it was in fact the Holy Spirit himself, who is called the oil of gladness because he is the source of spiritual joy. But we too have been anointed with oil, and by this anointing we have entered into fellowship with Christ and have received a share in his life. Beware of thinking that this holy oil is simply ordinary oil and nothing else. After the invocation of the Spirit it is no longer ordinary oil but the gift of Christ, and by the presence of his divinity it becomes the instrument through which we receive the Holy Spirit. While symbolically, on our foreheads and senses, our bodies are anointed with this oil that we see, our souls are sanctified by the holy and life-giving Spirit."[56]

In the Latin Church the sacrament of Confirmation has been set adrift from Baptism, largely as an accident of history. As was explained in the previous section, in the ancient Church the newly baptized were brought before the bishop for Chrismation or Confirmation. The Latin Church was keen to keep this living connection with the bishop and delayed Confirmation until the bishop could get to a particular Church. Baptism, however, was not delayed and the relatively small number of bishops and the large number of converts resulted in Baptism and Confirmation becoming more and more separated in time. Eventually, the stage was reached when baptism was normally received as an infant and Confirmation was not received until the person was an "adult" and a theology began to form which saw this as a desirable state of affairs.

In the Byzantine Church the connection between baptism and Chrismation was maintained and the two sacraments, though separate, were always seen as intimately connected. In this, the Byzantine Church has tried to remain as close as possible to the practice of the early Church. However, faced with the same practical problems as the Latin Church, compromises had to be made as the Church grew. In the Byzantine Church the impossibility of a few bishops confirming a large number of new Christians, both adults and infants, in a timely manner (and the undesirability of a prolonged postponement to baptism) was solved by allowing the local priest to administer the sacrament of Chrismation with the connection to the Bishop being maintained through the consecration of the oil. Chrismation can

---

56   *St. Cyril of Jerusalem, Cat. 21 Mystagogica 3, 1-3 PG 33. 1087-109.*

only be administered with oil especially blessed for that purpose by the bishop. This re-expreses the connection to the bishop and the sacrament, and therefore to his people, and maintains the unity of Christian Initiation.

The procedure for Chrismation, or Confirmation, are the same in the Latin and Byzantine Churches. The candidate is anointed with specially blessed Chrism (myron), a fragrant oil, and hands are laid on them. It is true to say however, that in the Latin Church more emphasis is placed on the laying on of hands while the Byzantine Church places more emphasis on the anointing (hence the name Chrismation). This difference in emphasis probably has to do with the important connection between this sacrament and the bishop, a connection which goes back to apostolic times. In the Latin Church this connection is strongly maintained in the person of the bishop who lays his hands on each candidate, while in the Byzantine Church it is maintained by the oil used in anointing which is specially blessed for the purpose by the bishop.

While the Latin West has maintained the strong connection between the sacrament of Confirmation and the bishop, it has paid a high price for separating Confirmation from Baptism. The problem is that someone who has been baptized in infancy has been living as a Christian for many years, and has often been receiving the Eucharist for many years, before they are confirmed. This has led to something of a crisis in the western understanding of Confirmation which has been described as "a sacrament searching for a theology". The confusion was caused by the temporal separation of the two sacraments. This was compounded by the ambivalence of many Protestant Churches to infant Baptism and the dual meaning of the term 'confirmation'. In these Protestant usages, Confirmation is seen as an adult commitment to Christ – you confirm as an adult the promises made for you as an infant. Confirmation thus moves from a sacrament of initiation to a Christian teenage rite of passage. This theology has influenced Roman Catholic theology with many understanding Confirmation as giving the grace to become an "adult Christian". Confirmation became restricted, except in danger of death, to after the age of discernment (generally considered to be about seven years) and came to be considered as the sacrament of "Christian maturity". The practice grew of delaying Confirmation until the teenage years[57].

Never-the-less, the Latin Church still insists on the unity of the sacraments of Christian initiation and rejects any understanding of these sacraments which separates them. Confirmation completes the initiation of the Christian begun at Baptism and it is certainly not to be understood as an adult validation of the promises made for the infant as Baptism – although this does occur as a precursor to the sacrament in order to remind the candidates of the unity of the two sacraments.

---

57   Following Vatican II, this trend has been reversed in many Latin Dioceses by reuniting Confirmation and the reception of First Holy Communion.

The word confirmation is not to be understood here as "I confirm this commitment" but rather in the sense of "to establish more firmly, to ratify and make formally valid."[58] It has an overtone of strength as when a horse breeder speaks of the "solid confirmation" of a race horse. He means that the horse is well built for speed and power. The key difference between these two understandings is that in the orthodox catholic understanding, it is the Holy Spirit who confirms the Christian – Latin or Byzantine. It is He who strengthens them and establishes them more firmly in the Christian life, rather than it being the Christian who is *confirming* their commitment.

To emphasis the unity of the sacrament, the Second Vatican Council directed that; *"The rite of Confirmation is to be revised also so that the intimate connection of this sacrament with the whole of Christian Initiation may more clearly appear"*[59]. The Rite of Christian Initiation of Adults (RCIA) restored the full unity of these sacraments, with Confirmation administered by the baptizing priest, in a manner similar to the practice of the Byzantine Church. However, since most Christians are baptized as infants, the sacramental theology of the Latin Church is still separated from its ritual expression in the life of the Church. This can lead to confusion, especially in societies dominated by protestant traditions.

The Byzantine Church has never separated these two sacraments and so has never suffered from this confusion. It remains understood in the same way as it was understood in the early Church (as the sacrament which completes baptism and seals the new Christian with, and brings about the full indwelling and grace of, the Holy Spirit) and this understanding is expressed in its ritual practice.

As always, the Byzantine Church expresses its theology of Christian Initiation in an Icon. In this case the icon of Christian Initiation is the Baptism of Christ which shows not only John the Baptist pouring water over Christ's head in the act of baptism but also the Spirit descending from the Father to "anoint" Christ for his mission. In the lower right there is a small figure with an axe standing next to a tree. This symbolizes that the old order is about to be cut down, (the axe has been laid to roots of the tree) and that the Christian will now enter into a new order of creation. The unity and fullness of Christian Initiation is here expressed in the icon, since not only are the gospel origins of Baptism and Chrismation shown, but the Eucharist is also prefigured. Here, at the start of his public life, Christ is giving himself to the world. He is starting on the road which will lead to his crucifixion and resurrection.

Lord, when You were baptized in the Jordan, the veneration of the Trinity was revealed. For the voice of the Father gave witness to You, calling You Beloved, and the Spirit, in the guise of a dove, confirmed the certainty of His words. Glory to You, Christ our God, who appeared and enlightened the world.

Troparion of the Epiphany

---

58   The Concise Oxford Dictionary
59   Sacrosanctum Concillium

Traditional Festal Icon of the Baptism of Christ

Eucharist - Fire in the cup

*"The place where you shall presently stand after your baptism before the great
sanctuary is a foretype of the future glory. The psalmody with which you will
be received is a prelude to the psalmody of Heaven; the lamps which you will
kindle are a sacrament of the illumination there with which we shall meet the
Bridegroom, ... "*[60]

Stepping off from St Gregory's reference we can draw closer to understanding the
Eucharist, the deepest mystery at the heart of the Church. In the Eucharist the Church
not only joins itself to Christ in his death and resurrection, but comes with him into
the presence of the Father and joins in tasting the first fruits of the heavenly banquet,
fed on that blossom and fruit of the Tree of Life, the Cross of Jesus.

On the notice board outside the front door of Sts Peter and Paul's Ukrainian
Catholic Cathedral in Melbourne (an Eastern Catholic Church of the Byzantine
Rite), there are a series of notices explaining the differences between the Latin
and Byzantine Rites of the Catholic Church – presumably for visiting and curious
Latin Rite Catholics. These notices do not talk about differences in Eucharistic
theology but rather differences in liturgical practice. It is an interesting choice
and seems to be predicated on an understanding that the disputes in Eucharistic
theology between the two traditions are small and subtle and in themselves give
no indication of the life of either Church. When dealing with differences which are
primarily differences of emphasis and nuance, as we are in eucharistic theology,
then the celebration of the Liturgy is the best window into the understanding of the
respective Churches.

The comparisons given can be summarized as follows: in the Latin Church, and
with the liturgical reforms of Vatican II, the Eucharist is seen as the people of God
gathered around the table of the Lord and looks to the model of the last supper.
However in the Byzantine Church the celebration is seen as leading the people to
participate in the heavenly liturgy of God's Kingdom. It takes the heavenly liturgy
as its model. The Latin Church's liturgy is thus simple, with a relatively frugal use
of symbols. It promotes clear messages with a "down to earth" atmosphere and
sees beauty in simplicity. The Byzantine Liturgy on the other hand makes full use
of all the senses and uses symbols extensively to promote a more mystical, holistic
understanding which comes from the deepest part of the self. Its focus is on cosmic
realities and eschatology. It seeks to make heaven present on Earth, celebrating
with an emphasis on beauty.

---

60   Instruction to Catecumens, Oration 40 of St. Gregory of Nazianus

This simple comparison is perhaps drawing too sharp a line and opposing end points without looking at the fullness of practice in each of the traditions. It is, however, a useful summary and indication of the differences in approach. The notices go on to point out that these approaches are not truly in opposition, but are complimentary. Together they express the fullness and variety of God's Church.

In particular, it should be noted that the elements emphasized in one tradition are not totally absent from the other. While the model of the Eucharist as a sacramental meal, as a participation in the last supper of Christ, is prominent in the Latin Church's liturgy, it is by no means absent from the understanding of the Byzantine Church. Consider the following hymn by St. Ephraem the Syrian in praise of the upper room where the last supper was celebrated;

"Blessed are you O place, which no human being saw nor sees what you saw. Our Lord, as he is made the altar of justice, Priest and bread and cup of salvation. That is to say, in his substance he is sufficient for all. It is impossible that another one would be sufficient for it. Altar and lamb, sacrifice and sacrificer, priest and the one fit to be food. Blessed are you, o place, never was prepared [a table] like your table among kings. also not in the tent of the Holy of Holies, on account of which the shew-bread was prepared. It was you [in] which first was broken that bread; so that you [o place] came to be its Church. First-born of altars, which went first in his Eucharist, in you it appeared first.⁶¹ "

The sacrifice of the last supper is not seen as separate from the sacrifice on Calvary. Rather, it is the same sacrifice in anticipation. In the upper room Christ offers himself for us by his own hand and makes it clear that he is both the priest and the willing victim in the sacrifice of Calvary. This unity between the sacramental sacrifice of the last supper and the physical sacrifice on Golgotha is also well expressed in the hymns of St. Ephraem:

It was the very same Christ in the Upper Room who gave and was distributed to all. Even though the people slew him, he had previously slain himself with his own hand. It was one slain by his own hands that the crazed ones crucified on Golgotha; had he not slain himself in symbol, they would not have slain Him in actual fact.⁶²

and also:

He broke the bread with his own hands in a mystic sign of the sacrifice of his body. He mixed the cup with his own hands in a mystic sign of the sacrifice of his blood. He offered up himself in sacrifice, the priest of our atonement.⁶³

---

61   *Armenian Hymns* 48, lines 41-48. As quoted in C.B. Horn, *Fire and the Holy Spirit in the Bread and in the Cup,* Orientale Lumen, Australasia – Oceania 2000, Australian Catholic University, Melbourne, 2000, p136.
62   Hymns of the Unleavened Bread 2:7 As quoted in C.B. Horn, *Fire and the Holy Spirit in the Bread and in the Cup,* Orientale Lumen, Australasia – Oceania 2000, Australian Catholic University, Melbourne, 2000, p141.
63   ibid.

It is this union between the celebration of the Eucharist and the sacrifice on Calvary that gives life to the Church. The Church is constantly standing with Mary in the presence of the cross and being nourished by the blood flowing from his side – just as it is constantly standing in the transcendent glory of the resurrection. When a group of early martyrs were offered their lives if only they would refrain from celebrating the Eucharist, they replied that this was impossible since the Eucharist was life to them.

This idea is also expressed in the traditional icon of the crucifixion. The water and blood are seen flowing from his side like a fountain, while blood also runs down onto a skull lying in a dark hole at the foot of the cross. The skull represents Adam, man, who is lying dead and lost in the darkness of sin. The blood of Christ is flowing down from the cross to give life to these dry bones. There are multiple

11th century Greek mosaic of the crucifixion.

references here to the whole story of salvation; from the creation narrative where Eve was clothed in flesh from a bone taken from Adam's body; to the Passover in Egypt where the blood of a lamb saved the Hebrews, to the prophetic vision in Ezekiel where the dry bones of God's people are given life and breath again and clothed once more in flesh.[64]

All of creation and all of salvation history reaches its climax on Golgotha and it is this which is made present in the Eucharist.

St John Chrysostom puts it this way:

If we wish to understand the power of Christ's blood, we should go back to the ancient account of its prefiguration in Egypt. "Sacrifice a lamb without blemish", commanded Moses, "and sprinkle its blood on your doors". If we were to ask him what he meant, and how the blood of an irrational beast could possibly save men endowed with reason, his answer would be that the saving power lies not in the blood itself, but in the fact that it is a sign of the Lord's blood. In those days, when the destroying angel saw the blood on the doors he did not dare to enter, so how much less will the devil approach now when he sees, not that figurative blood on the doors, but the true blood on the lips of believers, the doors of the temple of Christ.

If you desire further proof of the power of this blood, remember where it came from, how it ran down from the cross, flowing from the Master's side. The gospel records that when Christ was dead, but still hung on the cross, a soldier came and pierced his side with a lance and immediately there poured out water and blood. Now the water was a symbol of baptism and the blood, of the holy Eucharist. The soldier pierced the Lord's side, he breached the wall of the sacred temple, and I have found the treasure and made it my own. So also with the lamb: the Jews sacrificed the victim and I have been saved by it.

"There flowed from his side water and blood". Beloved, do not pass over this mystery without thought; it has yet another hidden meaning, which I will explain to you. I said that water and blood symbolized baptism and the holy Eucharist. From these two sacraments the Church is born: from baptism, "the cleansing water that gives rebirth and renewal through the Holy Spirit", and from the holy Eucharist. Since the symbols of baptism and the Eucharist flowed from his side, it was from his side that Christ fashioned the Church, as he had fashioned Eve from the side of Adam Moses gives a hint of this when he tells the story of the first man and makes him exclaim: "Bone from my bones and flesh from my flesh!" As God then took a rib from Adam's side to fashion a woman, so Christ has given us blood and water from his side to fashion the Church. [65]

---

64   Ezekiel 37,1-14
65   St. John Chrysostom, Instructions to Catecumens. CAT 3

Given this identity between the sacramental sacrifice of the Eucharist and the physical sacrifice on Calvary, the real presence of Christ in the Eucharist has always been accepted by the Byzantine Church and it has never been a source of contention between the Latin and Byzantine Churches in the way that it has between the Latin Church and the Protestant Traditions.

Do not, then, regard the Eucharistic elements as ordinary bread and wine: they are in fact the body and blood of the Lord, as he himself has declared. Whatever your senses may tell you, be strong in faith. You have been taught and you are firmly convinced that what looks and tastes like bread and wine is not bread and wine but the body and the blood of Christ. You know also how David referred to this long ago when he sang: Bread gives strength to man's heart and makes his face shine with the oil of gladness. Strengthen your heart, then, by receiving this bread as spiritual bread, and bring joy to the face of your soul[66].

Each Church believes that in a mysterious way and through the power of the Holy Spirit, the bread and wine really become the Body and Blood of Christ, although each Church has approached the mystery in different ways. The Latin Church, since the time of St. Thomas Aquinas, has spoken of transubstantiation where the ontological reality, the substance, of the bread and wine are changed, but the appearances, the accidents, remain the same. While the Byzantine Church will also use this language at times, it emphasizes that it is by way of description only and it is wary of the neo-Aristotelian thought that lies behind it. This seems to imply a scientific delving into the process through which God's Spirit acts – a delving that would at best be foolish and at worst even a sacrilegious denial of the divine mystery. To the western mind, of course, accurate description, careful definition and logical analysis do not deny the mystery, but are tools in coming to an appreciation of it. The eastern mind, which seeks a more synthesized, holistic understanding, remains deeply suspicious of such an approach. This approach is very well summed up in the writings of St. John Damascene, nearly 500 years before St. Thomas Aquinas:

You ask how the bread becomes the Body of Christ, and how the wine...the Blood of Christ. I shall tell you; the Holy Spirit comes upon them and accomplishes what surpasses every word and thought...Let it be enough for you to understand that it is by the Holy Spirit, just as it was of the Holy Virgin and by the Holy Spirit that the Lord, through and in himself, took flesh[67].

St. John Damascene in this passage links the Eucharist to the feast of the

---

66   St. Cyril of Jerusalem *Catecheses,* Lecture 22, ss. 1,3-6,9
67   St. John Damascene, De fide orth. 4, 13. As quoted in *The Catechism of the Catholic Church.* The inclusion of this quote in what is, essentially, a document of the Latin Church indicates how close the two Churches are in their understanding of the Eucharist. It is also possible to read this as indicating the extent to which the Latin Church has, without compromising its own theology, adopted the Byzantine rather than scholastic understanding of the Eucharist.

Annunciation and the Incarnation. Indeed, it is not possible to separate the Eucharist and the Incarnation – in both of these the Divine Word of God becomes present in the matter of creation and all creation is divinized. The connections here are deep. At the Annunciation, the Spirit hovered over Mary, the mother and archetype of the Church, and the Divine Word became enfleshed in her womb. At each celebration of the Eucharist, the Spirit hovers over the offerings of the Church and the Divine Word enters into the physical matter of our world. It is the Spirit who brings about Christ's presence in obedience to the will of the Father. Bishop Kallistos Ware sums up this connection in two passages from his book *The Orthodox Way*[68]:

At the Annunciation the Holy Spirit descends upon the Virgin Mary, and she conceives the Logos: according to the creed, Jesus Christ was "incarnate from the Holy Spirit and the Virgin Mary". Here it is the Spirit sending Christ into the world.[69]

And

As at the Annunciation, so in the extension of Christ's Incarnation at the Eucharist, the Father sends down the Holy Spirit, to effect the Son's presence in the consecrated gifts. Here, as always, the three persons of the Trinity are working together.[70]

While the fact of the real presence was never a matter of dispute between the Latin and Byzantine Churches, the exact moment within the liturgy when this transformation takes place was a matter of great dispute, although the dispute only arose after and as a result of the liturgical analysis of scholastic theologians. The dispute revolved around the role of the epiclesis and the words of institution in the liturgy. The Byzantine Church, with its reverence for the Holy Spirit, has always placed great emphasis on the epiclesis, the calling on the Father to send the Holy Spirit to hover over the gifts of bread and wine, since it was through the power of the Spirit that these gifts were changed into the body and blood of Christ. The Latin Church with its greater Christological focus, on the other hand, placed enormous emphasis on the words of institution: this is my body, this is my blood - to the extent that the Tridentine Liturgy had no clear epiclesis, although it is implied, though earlier western liturgies certainly did have an epiclesis. In some ways this dispute was driven by extremists on both sides with calmer heads holding that the whole of the Eucharistic prayer was important. The liturgical changes in the Latin Church following Vatican II reinstated a clear epiclesis into the western liturgy, although it is placed before the words of institution rather than following them as it is in the Byzantine Liturgy.

The distance that the Latin Church has moved from any possible over emphasis

---

68   These two passages are not linked in the original book. The linkage is the current author's.
69   Ware, K. 1995, *The Orthodox Way*, St. Vladimir's seminary Press, New York, P92.
70   Ibid, P37.

on the words of institution can be seen fully in its recognition of the validity of the Anaphora of Addai and Mari – the Eucharistic rite of the Assyrian Church of the East which is notable because, from time immemorial, it has been used without a recitation of the institution narrative but with an explicit epiclesis. As the Latin Church has always placed such stress on the words of the Eucharistic Institution, and considered them to be a constitutive and therefore indispensable part of the Eucharistic Prayer, a long and careful study was undertaken of the Anaphora of Addai and Mari, from a historical, liturgical and theological perspective. The result of this study was that the Congregation for the Doctrine of Faith, (under the then Cardinal Ratzinger, now pope emeritus Benedict XVI) on January 17th 2001 concluded that this Anaphora can be considered perfectly valid. Pope John Paul II approved this decision. The reasons given were based on the ancient heritage of this Eucharistic prayer and the apostolic descent of the Assyrian Church. The Congregation went further, however, and made the following statement: *"the words of Eucharistic Institution are indeed present in the Anaphora of Addai and Mari, not in a coherent narrative way and ad litteram, but rather in a dispersed euchological way, that is, integrated in successive prayers of thanksgiving, praise and intercession."* (Congregation for the Doctrine of Faith, Rome, July 20th, 2001)

There is a contrast here between a liturgy (the Tridentine) which has a very unclear and dispersed epiclesis but a very clear emphasis on the words of institution with an ancient liturgy (the Anaphora of Addai and Mari) which has a clear epiclesis but no coherent narrative of the words of institution - both are considered valid. Underlying this statement is a recognition that it is the Holy Spirit who brings about the transformation of the bread and wine into the body and blood of Christ. He does this within the context of the faithful, Eucharistic Church community and apostolic tradition. It is the action of the Spirit within the Church which brings about this most marvelous transformation – not the form of words alone. Sacraments, no matter how miraculous their effect, are never magic. A priest is not a magician.

The Eucharist is unique among the sacraments of initiation in that it is the only one which can be received more than once. While the common frequency of communion has varied from time in each of the Churches, and often varies between the Churches, weekly reception of the Eucharist has traditionally been considered the norm of Christian life. At times in the Latin Church, daily reception has been promoted as the ideal and even, in the tridentine Church, mandated for priests. So, how can a sacrament which many Christians receive every week be considered a Sacrament of Initiation?

In the Byzantine Church, as in the ancient Church, the Eucharist is the last of the three Sacraments of Initiation to be received. These sacraments are received sequentially but as part of the same rite of initiation. The Catechumens were first washed of their sins and born into new life through the waters of Baptism. They then had hands laid upon them and were anointed with chrism to be sealed and commissioned as Christians in the Spirit and to be given the grace and power that they needed to live their new life by the Spirit. It is then that they are taken for the first time to the celebration of the Eucharist to receive the body and blood of Christ which was first given for them on Calvary. In doing so, not only do they receive the spiritual food they need for their new life but, through the Spirit, they enter into profound communion with Christ himself. Christ enters into the depths of their being and they become a part of Him through His mystical body – the Church.

Moses gives a hint of this when he tells the story of the first man and makes him exclaim: "Bone from my bones and flesh from my flesh!" As God then took a rib from Adam's side to fashion a woman, so Christ has given us blood and water from his side to fashion the Church[71].

and also;

In a new way, his body is kneaded into our bodies. And his pure blood is poured out into our veins, his voice into our ears, his brightness into our eyes. All of him is kneaded into all of us by his compassion. And since he loved his Church very much, He did not give her the manna of her rival – He himself became the living bread for her to eat.[72]

The role of the Eucharist in the Rite of Christian Initiation is thus clear: Baptism, Chrismation and Eucharist are all part of the same event of becoming: of bringing to life a new Christian. This is beautifully expressed by Ephraem the Syrian in his Hymn on Faith:

Behold, Fire and Spirit in the womb of her who bore you; Behold, Fire and Spirit in the river in which you were baptized. Fire and Spirit in our baptismal font. And in the bread and cup – Fire and Holy Spirit.[73]

There is a direct analogy here with natural human birth. A baby is born through the breaking of the placental waters. It is then held until the doctor or midwife ensures that it draws its first breath. The new baby is then placed on its mother's breast and draws the nourishment and strength it needs from her body. In this process the baby has passed from its previous limited existence into a new life, full of unexplored possibilities. The parallel with the sacraments of Christian initiation is clear: we are born into new life in Baptism, we breath in the Holy Spirit in Chrismation and we are fed the body and blood of Christ by our mother, the Church. We are indeed *"born again of water and the Holy Spirit"* and leave our old, limited lives to enter

---

71   St. John Chrysostom, Instructions to Catecumens. CAT 3
72   *Hymns on Virginity* 37:2 As quoted in C.B. Horn, *Fire and the Holy Spirit in the Bread and in the Cup*, Orientale lumen, Australasia – Oceania 2000, Australian Catholic University, Melbourne, 2000, p151.
73   *Hymns on Faith* 10:17 As quoted in C.B. Horn, *Fire and the Holy Spirit in the Bread and in the Cup*, Orientale lumen, Australasia – Oceania 2000, Australian Catholic University, Melbourne, 2000, p147.

a new existence full of unexplored, and undreamt of possibilities.

This mirror of the sequence of childbirth is not accidental, nor is it something read into the rite at some later date. It is deliberate and intended. Consider the following from St John Chrysostom:

"Do you understand, then, how Christ has united his bride to himself and what food he gives us all to eat? By one and the same food we are both brought into being and nourished. As a woman nourishes her child with her own blood and milk, so does Christ unceasingly nourish with his own blood those to whom he himself has given life."[74]

In the Latin Church, where Confirmation came to be delayed and received in late childhood, the order in which the sacraments of initiation were received was changed so that a child often, indeed normally, received First Holy Communion before Confirmation. As was discussed earlier, the fathers of Vatican II took steps to rectify this anomaly, but it has become entrenched Church practice. This separation of the sacraments, and the change in their order, destroyed the parallel with natural human birth and meant that the intimate connection of the three sacraments, in the one event of becoming a new Christian, was obscured. Yet even in these circumstances, the Eucharist retained its character as a sacrament of initiation. It did this not just in theory or academic theology, but in actual Church practice and popular piety. The social practices and customs which surround a child's first Holy Communion throughout the Latin Church, in all its various cultures, are ample evidence of the persistent sense and understanding of the faithful people of God that the Eucharist is indeed a sacrament of initiation.

Does this mean therefore that there are two sacraments; the first Eucharist which is combined with Baptism and Chrismation in the rite of Christian initiation and the normal Eucharist which we would receive every week? Of course not. There is only one sacrament of the Eucharist in which, by the power of the Holy Spirit, we participate in the one sacrifice of Calvary and in which we receive Christ in all His fullness. What then does it mean that we receive one of the sacraments of initiation every week? There is a sense in which our initiation as Christians is never complete. We are always coming into the fullness of the new life given by Christ. The Spirit who makes Christ present to us in the Eucharist is continually transforming us, just as He transforms the bread and wine, to become like Christ – to enter into the divine life. In the Byzantine Church, as in the Catholic tradition of the western Church, Christian life is a process of growth, a gradual process of becoming divine. There is not the sense that becoming a Christian involves a simple declaration of faith and that's the end of it – as there tends to be in some evangelical traditions. It is entirely appropriate therefore that Christians should be

---

74   St John Chrysostom, Instructions to Catecumens, CAT 3

continually initiated into the mystery of Christ made present to them by the Spirit.

In coming into the closest possible union with Christ, the people of God are also brought into union with each other. This constitutes the fundamental unity of the Church constitutes; that we are all members of the one mystical body of Christ. In the Eucharist we are called together by the Word, formed into the Body of Christ by the Spirit and brought to the presence of the Father. It is here that the Church is most fully herself, mystically united across time and space in the worship of God. It is this mystical union which finds its expression in Holy Communion and it is entirely appropriate that the Rite of Christian Initiation concludes with the new Christian entering into this communion for the first time.

In Communion we come most intimately into the presence of Christ and his presence within us transforms us; not only uniting us with our fellow Christians but changing us so that we become like Christ. Indeed, we are made into Christ. As the bread and wine are changed through the action of the Spirit into Christ's body and blood during the prayer of consecration, so by the same Spirit are we changed into Christ in Holy Communion.

May purity of conscience remove the veil from the face of your soul so that be contemplating the glory of the Lord, as in a mirror, you may be transformed from glory to glory in Christ Jesus our Lord. To him be glory for ever and ever. Amen.

It is indeed the destiny of the Christian to be transformed from glory to glory by the Spirit, to be made more and more Christ-like until we, in union with all of creation, stand before the throne of the Father and cry *Glory!* This is the journey started at baptism, this journey to divinity, to a participation in the life of the Trinity. The bread and wine which were made by human hands to sustain us in our everyday journeys are marvelously changed to become the mystical food we need for a journey to the very depths of what is real. Our bodies take the normal food and change it into the energy we need for our everyday lives. The food of the Eucharist takes our normal bodies and makes them divine by gift and participation, it makes our whole being shine with the life and Spirit of God. It is then that our Christian Initiation is complete.

As Bishop Kallistos Ware makes clear, the Eucharist is the pinnacle of Christian life.

Earlier we noted...how the whole of the ascetic and mystical life is already contained in the sacrament of Baptism: however far a person advances upon the Way, all that he discovers is nothing else than the revelation or making manifest of Baptismal grace. The same can be said of Holy Communion: the whole of the ascetic and mystical life is a deepening and realization of our Eucharistic union with Christ the Saviour...It is above all through Communion that the Christian is made one with and in Christ, "christified", "ingoded" or 'deified", it is above all through Communion that he receives the first fruits of eternity. "Blessed is he that has eaten the bread of love which is Jesus," writes St. Isaac the Syrian. "While still in this world he breaths the air of resurrection in which the righteous will delight after they rise from the dead." "All human striving reaches here its ultimate goal," says Nicholas Cabisilas. "For in this sacrament we attain God himself, and God himself is made one with us in the most perfect of all possible unions...This is the final mystery: beyond this it is not possible to go, not can anything be added to it."[75]

---

75   Ware, K. 1995, *The Orthodox Way*, St. Vladimir's seminary Press, New York, P109.

Reconciliation – The Father's Loving Embrace

Through heedlessness I have fallen into the heavy sleep of sin. But, my Christ, who for my sake hast fallen asleep on the cross, do thou awaken me, that the night of death comes not upon me[76].

A tale comes to us from the tradition of the desert fathers about a curious stranger who asked one of the desert monks; "What do you monks do all day out there in the desert?" The monk relied, "We fall down and we get up again. We fall down and we get up again." There are surprising depths in this deceptively simple answer. The monks went into the desert to live the fullest expression of the Christian life and so the monk might have been expected to talk about prayer, fasting and meditation – all things that the monks of the desert most certainly did do. The monk, however, mentions none of these things. Instead he talks about sin and repentance as the two central facts of a monk's (and therefore of a Christian's) life. The desert tradition sees sin as a constant part of Christian life and to live a Christian life well is not to be free of sin (since this is impossible) but to repent as often as we sin. Since we sin constantly we must repent constantly. Since the depth of human sin is great, our repentance must be great. This is why Abba Sisoes could cry out at the end of his life, "It seems to me I have not yet begun to repent[77]." A cry which astounded the monks gathered around their revered and honoured Abba and yet one which convinced them further of his holiness. Repentance, not sinlessness, is the normal mark of holiness[78]. This is why St Isaias of Sketis said, "*God requires us to go on repenting until our last breath[79].*" And why St. Isaac the Syrian said, "*This life has been given to you for repentance. Do not waste it on other things[80].*"

To live a life of constant repentance may seem rather gloomy and yet there is no hint of despair in the monks reply to the curious stranger. Indeed, it is a light hearted answer. It is the answer of a man who knows that however often he sins, he will be given the grace to repent and that it is his repented sins which will bring him closer to God – and not to some pretended holiness. This is the foundation of the sacrament of Penance, also known as Confession or Reconciliation. It is not primarily the removal of sin-built barriers to the grace of God, although it does of

---

76 Irmos of the Eighth Canticle of Matins, First Friday of Lent.

77 see *The Sayings of the Desert Fathers*, Book ii. *In The Desert Fathers*, Tr by Helen Waddell, Random House, New York, 1998.

78 The only exceptions to this rule are the divine Word made flesh, Jesus of Nazareth, and his holy mother, Mary.

79 St Isaias of Sketis, Ascetical Homilies, xvi, 11, ed. Monk Avgoustinos, Jerusalem, 1911, p100. as quoted in Ware, K. 1995, *The Orthodox Way*, St. Vladimir's seminary Press, New York, P114.

80 St Isaac the Syrian, Ascetical Homilies 74 (79), tr Holy Transfiguration Monastery, p364, as quoted in Ware, K. 1995, *The Orthodox Way*, St. Vladimir's seminary Press, New York, P114.

course do that, but rather it brings our sins before Christ so that they are forgiven and transformed. It is our repented sinfulness itself that becomes our means of spiritual growth and a proper understanding of repentance is necessary for a proper understanding of the sacrament of Penance.

A life of repentance is therefore joyful rather than gloomy. The tears of sorrow at sin and the suffering it causes are also tears of joy because of the grace, the mercy and the love of God. In the west repentance has come to be associated with self-loathing and has acquired many negative connotations. This association comes from a rather Protestant view of salvation where human nature is utterly corrupt and depraved and thus totally dependent on the grace of God. In this view, repentance involves facing the depths of your own corruption. Without a solid understanding of faith and grace this can quickly descend into a very negative view of humanity. This is not the view of the Byzantine Church which has always seen human nature as graced from its creation in the image of God, disfigured by the fall and by sin and in need a the healing grace of God, but fundamentally good nonetheless. Repentance is thus associated with healing rather than self-loathing. This association with healing comes directly from the gospels and it means that repentance has a fundamentally positive connotation.

Bishop Kallistos Ware describes the Eastern Church's understanding of repentance in the following way:

Repentance marks the starting point of our journey. The Greek term Metanoia *... signifies primarily a "change of mind". Correctly understood, repentance is not negative but positive. It means not self-pity or remorse but conversion, the re-centering of our whole life on the Trinity. It is to look not backward with regret but forward with hope – not downwards at our shortcomings but upwards at God's love. It is to see, not what we have failed to be, but what by divine grace we can now become; and it is to act on what we see. To repent is to open our eyes to the light. In this sense, repentance is not just a single act, an initial step, but a continuing state, an attitude of heart and will that needs to be ceaselessly renewed up to the end of life[81].*

Stories of healing are a major feature of all the Gospels and in many of these stories Jesus will give the sick person something they haven't asked for – the forgiveness of their sins. Healing and forgiveness are linked from the very beginnings of Christianity and this link is important in a proper understanding of the sacrament of Penance. This is shown most clearly in the story of the paralytic at Capernaum who is lowered through the roof into the presence of Jesus[82]. When he sees the man, the first thing Jesus does, unasked for, is to tell him that his sins are forgiven. This

81   Ware, K. 1995, *The Orthodox Way*, St. Vladimir's Seminary Press, New York, P114.
82   Mt 9:2-8, Lk 5:17-26

is a direct challenge to the old Jewish order where sins could only be forgiven by making the appropriate sacrifice in the temple. Here, it is the person of Jesus Christ who forgives sin and the old order is done away with. Jesus then goes on to heal the man's physical infirmity as a sign of his authority. Since sin and sickness (or misfortune) were strongly linked in Jewish thought, this healing was a powerful sign of Christ's authority.

There are a number of important lessons that we can learn about the sacrament of Penance from this story. The first is that the man was brought into Jesus' presence by his friends, who lowered him through the roof, and it was because of **their** faith that Jesus could heal and forgive the man. In the same way, we come to Jesus in this sacrament through the Church and it is the faith of our Church which makes the sacrament possible. We receive this sacramental forgiveness as a member of the Church. The second thing to notice is that it is the person of Jesus Christ who forgives sin. The Church's role is to bring us into the presence of Christ. The third lesson is to do with authority. Christ clearly intended this healing to be a sign of His authority to forgive sins - "to prove to you that the son of man has authority on earth to forgive sins…". He claims this authority, and in doing so He proclaims that the old order is passing away and that the new order is established in His person.

The Church has always understood that this authority was passed on to the Apostles. The clearest reference is in the Gospel of John where Christ appears to the disciples after the resurrection and, in formal ceremony, says to them:

"…receive the Holy Spirit. For those whose sins you forgive they are forgiven; for those whose sins you retain, they are retained."[83]

This echoes the previous promise of authority given to Peter and his fellow apostles;

"I will give you the keys of the kingdom of heaven: whatever you bind on earth shall be considered bound in heaven; whatever you loose on earth shall be considered loosed in heaven."[84]

The signs given here are formal and legal. The keys were the traditional sign of the authority given to a steward to act in his master's place (usually worn on the shoulder) and the terms used for *to bind* and *to loose* are technical rabbinical terms relating to excommunication[85]. The passages, not only in their words but also in their formal setting, are clearly intended to show an explicit transfer of authority over sin.

While the early Church accepted that the apostles, and the bishops who were their

---

83   Jn 20:19-23
84   Mt 16:19
85   Kucharek, C. Sacramental Mysteries: A Byzantine Approach, Alleluia press, 1976, Ch XVII

successors, had the power to bind and to loose, there was no formal sacrament of reconciliation as we currently understand it. Instead, confession meant public confession and was only undertaken after serious sin, usually of such a public nature that it was likely to cause scandal. After such a sin, the sinner would have to endure a prolonged period of excommunication from the Church during which time they would be required to practice serious, onerous and sincere penance before they would be readmitted to the community. In many communities this could only happen once in your lifetime, leading to a perhaps understandable reluctance on the part of some sinners to undergo the process early.

This practice developed in the context of the Roman Empire's persecution of the Church - where many died a martyr's death but others betrayed their faith and, often, their community. Those who had betrayed their faith were viewed as traitors. They were dangerous and their re-admittance to the community was literally a matter of life and death. Against this background it was understandable that the Church community needed to be reassured of the penitent's sincerity. This led to a very rigorous understanding of Confession which persisted long after the persecution had stopped.

You might ask; what about the small, day to day sins – not the big scandals but the mean, little sins that are the stuff of normal Christian life? Here it is important to remember that Baptism is the primary sacrament for the forgiveness of sin and the reconciliation of the Christian with God, which is why Confession is sometimes referred to as "the second Baptism" in the Eastern Church. The waters of this "second baptism" are the tears of repentance shed by the sinner and these tears play an important role in the spiritual understanding of the Eastern Church. This connection between the waters of baptism and the tears of repentance was perhaps best spelt out in the writings of St Symeon the New theologian

Through holy baptism we are granted remission of our sins, are freed from the ancient curse, and are sanctified by the presence of the Holy Spirit....if after we have been baptized we gravitate towards evil and foul actions...through repentance, confession and tears we receive a corresponding remission of our former sins..[86]

..without tears our hardened hearts cannot be mollified, our souls cannot acquire spiritual humility[87].

The idea that tears of repentance heal our souls and restore our innocence was further developed by Nikitas Stithatos, a disciple and biographer of St. Symeon, who wrote extensively on prayer and the life of the spirit.

86   St Symeon the New Theologian, *One Hundred and Fifty-Three practical and Theological Texts*, No. 74. As quoted in The Philokalia, Vol. 4, Palmer, G.E.H., Sherrard, P. and K. Ware (trans.) Faber and Faber, London, 1995. p40.

87   ibid No.69, p39.

Sorrow prompted by God is an excellent tonic for those parts of the soul corrupted by evil actions and it restores them to their natural state. It dissolves through tears the storm clouds of passion and sin...[88]

...then with tears and a contrite heart once more offer your gift of prayer to the Father of the spiritual powers, and a righteous spirit will be renewed within you[89].

Sin after Baptism takes place in the context of the great, divine drama of the sacramental life of the Church and the transformation of the cosmos. As part of this divine drama, all the sacraments, when celebrated with the proper attitude, have the effect of forgiving sin. The Eucharist is especially important in this regard. The basis of this understanding is the gospel story of the woman with persistent internal bleeding (Luke 8; 40-48). In a mere touch of Christ's clothing she was healed and Christ turned to her and forgave her sins. In the Eucharist we do much more than just touch his garment. We receive Him fully and completely so that, unless there is some serious barrier which makes the act of communion an unreal mockery, how could we not be healed and forgiven?

Nevertheless, the grime of daily sin sets up barriers to the full Christian life of grace and community, and the Church, both East and West, came to realize that there was a need for a process of ongoing reconciliation. It is here that the development of the sacrament of Confession follows a curious parallel history in both the Eastern and Western Church. In both Churches frequent, sacramental confession is a gift to the wider Church from the monastic life. In the east the practice was introduced by the monks of the desert, while in the west, at about the same time, it was the wandering Irish monks who brought it to the wider Church[90]. In both cases the practice grew from people, both lay and priests, seeking out monks and hermits to act as what we would now term spiritual directors. These *geronda* (elders) in Greek or *anamchara* (friend of the soul) in Irish would meet with people and talk over their spiritual struggles and assure them of God's forgiveness. If the monks were priests (most were not) they would give sacramental absolution. It is in the monastic cell that the sacrament of Confession, as we currently understand it, was born.

This parallel development is a remarkable coincidence and it raises the question of whether or not there was some interaction between the two Churches. Did the Irish learn of the practice from the desert tradition, with which they certainly had a strong connection, or did wandering Irish monks introduce the practice to the east? There is no evidence either way, but it is remarkable that the two Churches, by

---

88   Nikitas Stithatos, *On the Practice of the Virtues,* As quoted in The Philokalia, Vol. 4, Palmer, G.E.H., Sherrard, P. and K. Ware (trans.) Faber and Faber, London, 1995. p95.

89   Nikitas Stithatos, *On the inner Nature of Things,* As quoted in The Philokalia, Vol. 4, Palmer, G.E.H., Sherrard, P. and K. Ware (trans.) Faber and Faber, London, 1995. p129.

90   It is ironic, but perhaps not surprising that the extremely ascetic Irish Church was the one which developed such an understanding not only of people's sinfulness but of the wide embrace of God's forgiveness. The same could be said of the monks of the desert.

now estranged from each other in both culture and theology, should develop such a similar form and understanding of the sacrament – although there are significant differences in practice and emphasis.

The practice of the Eastern Church in this celebration differs from that of the Latin Church and even, in detail, from Church to Church, particularly between the Slavonic and Hellenic Churches, although the main features are common. There is no confessional as there is in the Latin Church, although some Churches will use a screen. Instead, confession takes place in front of the Iconostasis which emphasizes the public, liturgical context of the sacrament and its strong connection to the healing power of Christ present in the Eucharist. On a stand will be placed an icon, or the book of the gospels, and a cross. These are symbols of Christ really present and it is before these that confession is made. The priest either stands or sits, according to local custom, to one side and greets the penitent with following prayer:

Behold, my child, Christ stands here invisibly and receives your confession. Therefore be not ashamed nor afraid; conceal nothing from me, but tell me without hesitation everything you have done, and so you shall have pardon from Our Lord Jesus Christ. See, his holy icon is before us, and I am but a witness, bearing testimony before him of all the things which you have to say to me. But if you conceal anything, you shall have the greater sin. Take heed, therefore, lest having come to a physician, you depart unhealed.

Confession is then made, either unassisted or in question and answer form, while the priest gives advice and encouragement. At the conclusion of the confession the penitent either bows their head or kneels and the priest places his stole and his hands on the penitents head and gives the prayer of absolution. The placing of the stole on the penitents head represents the authority of the Church to bind and to loose, while the laying on of hands calls down the power of the Holy Spirit to heal and forgive. The penitent would then kiss the icon, cross and the priest's hand, and return to the congregation.

The Western Church in the Tridentine era (pre-Vatican II) built up a complex classification of different types of sins and appropriate penances. These built on the penitentiaries from much earlier eras. Sins were classified as either venial or mortal. A venial sin hampered but did not stop the life of grace in a person while a mortal sin was so serious as to be deadly (hence mortal): it killed off the life of God's grace in the Christian. Penitents coming to Confession were given long lists of potential sins against which to examine their consciences. While these may have been a help to people who needed to call to mind forgotten sins, they promoted an overly legalistic approach to the sacrament of Confession – a crime and retribution model of the sacrament which the post-Vatican II Church has abandoned as inappropriate.

The Eastern Church has never developed such lists or classifications, seeing sin as sin and all sin as a symptom of our underlying sinfulness and separation from God. In coming to the sacrament all sin would be forgiven, "*deliberate and indelibrate, remembered and long forgotten*", because the sinner was being reconciled to God. This does not mean that the confession of individual sins is not important, as the final part of the introductory prayer makes very clear, just that the listing of our sins is not the primary focus. Rather, it is the reconciliation of the sinner to Christ and his Church.

Since the Western Church has largely abandoned the use of such lists (although they are still used by some conservative groups) this may seem to be more of a historical rather than fundamental difference. It does, however, highlight one of the basic differences in approach to Penance between the Byzantine and Latin Churches. In the Latin Church our sins are seen as separating us from God and these sins need to be forgiven in order to bring about reconciliation. The Byzantine Church on the other hand sees that it is the sinner who needs to be forgiven and that the confessed sins are symptoms of our separation from God rather than its cause. In the view of the Byzantine Church, we are sinners and it is as sinners that we need to be reconciled to God. Our sins show the concrete way in which this sinfulness is manifested more than presenting a list of incidents where forgiveness is needed. Perhaps the difference could be summed up in this brief bur rather simplistic way. In the Byzantine Church our sins are forgiven because we are reconciled to God and his Church, while in the Latin Church we are reconciled to God and his Church because our sins have been forgiven.

Another of the differences in the approach of the Byzantine and Latin Churches concerns the role of the priest. In the Latin Church the priest stands in the person of Christ and on behalf of the Church, delivers Christ's forgiveness. When done well this represents a powerful, personal encounter between the penitent and Christ, but it is prone to dissolve into clerical ritualism if done poorly. In the Byzantine Church the role of the priest is not so much to stand in the person of Christ as to stand as the representative of the Church, and of the bishop in particular, and to bring the penitent into the presence of Christ symbolized by an icon or cross. In and by Christ made present through the Spirit, the penitent is healed and forgiven. In terms of the gospel story discussed above, the priest takes the role not so much as Christ, but more as one of the men lowering the paralytic into the presence of Christ.

This is not so much a difference in theology as a difference in practice and emphasis. Both Churches would hold that it is Christ, present through the action of the Spirit, who forgives sin. Both would also hold that this forgiveness is expressed through the Church which was specifically commissioned to bind and to loose. However, the way in which each Church expresses this belief is different. This difference in emphasis is shown in the prayers that each Church uses in the sacrament. The Latin

Church uses the following form:

Through the ministry of the Church may God grant you pardon and peace and I absolve you of your sins in the name + of the Father and of the Son and of the Holy Spirit.

The equivalent prayer in the Melkite Byzantine Church is as follows, but it shows clear western influence:

Our Lord and God Jesus Christ, who gave this command to His divine and holy disciples and apostles; to loose and to bind the sins of people, forgives you from on high, all your sins and offences. I, his unworthy servant, who have received from these Apostles the power to do the same, absolve you from all censures, in as much as I can and am able, according to your need of it. Moreover, I absolve you from all your sins which you have confessed before God and my unworthiness. In the name + of the Father, and of the Son, and the Holy Spirit. Amen[91].

The priest may use the following absolution, which makes the distinction clearer and is more authentically Byzantine:

God through Nathan the prophet forgave David his sins; and Peter shedding bitter tears over his denial; and the Adulteress weeping at his feet; and the Publican and the Prodigal Son. May this same God, through me, a sinner, forgive + you everything in this life and in the life to come. And may he make you stand uncondemned before his awesome judgment-seat, for he is blessed forever and ever. Amen[92]

It is always God who forgives sin. In this mystery his Church, which by the power of the Spirit is Christ still present in the world, looses the chains of sin that have bound the sinner's heart. God takes us in His arms as the father of the prodigal son embraced the returning wanderer. He forgives us and He heals us.

As was mentioned earlier, it is clear from the Gospel stories that there is a strong link between the sacrament of reconciliation and that of healing. When people came to Christ for healing he would normally first give them something that they hadn't asked for – forgiveness. In part this was because in the Jewish mind of the time there was a strong link between sickness and sin. If you fell ill, or indeed if any other disaster befell you, it was probably because you had sinned. This is a view that has been revived by various Pentecostal sects today. Jesus specifically repudiated this interpretation[93] but it was certainly in the minds of those who came to him for the healing of their various ailments. It was partly as a consequence of this that he would first need to reassure the sick that their sins were forgiven, so that what they saw as the root cause of their illness had passed, before they could be healed. The two

91   Byzantine Melkite Euchologion - St. Paul Printing Press, Jounieh, Lebanon, 1977, pp.47-48
92   ibid
93   Jn 9:37

things were linked in the understanding of the people. This is why his healing of the paralytic could be given as evidence of the power to forgive sin, even though to the modern mind they are quite distinct activities.

There is a deeper point here though, one which passes beyond ancient ideas of divine retribution and is very relevant to our living today. We often see a certain perverse glamour in sin. The lives of many celebrities are not only infamous, but a source of great entertainment for the readers of popular magazines. The immediate pleasure of the sin is often seen as disconnected from the long term consequences of that sin in a person's life. Thus it is seen as surprising that a rock star who has lived a hedonistic social life, should end up locked in loneliness, isolation and despair – even though this outcome would be predicted by the moral theology of all the world's major religions.

This is not God's view. We might see glamour and pleasure in sin, but God, who sees truly, sees only pain and suffering. To God, our sin is part of our suffering, part of our broken humanity which needs healing as well as forgiveness. This is an important point since it influences the way in which we see God as reacting to our sin. Often, seeing glamour in sin, we see God as angry that we have taken some illicit pleasure or advantage – a God who will seek retribution unless he is appeased. God's true reaction, however, is sorrow and concern that we, whom He loves, have harmed ourselves. His desire is to forgive and heal. A proper understanding of what happens in the sacrament of Reconciliation is not us begging some measure of mercy from God for our sins, but rather us allowing God to break through the self-built dam of our sin to flood us with His loving mercy.

Sin is a symptom of our separation from God and it is our separation from God that causes all our grief and suffering. This means that it is not enough for the sacrament of reconciliation to forgive sin since our underlying separation would remain. The simple forgiveness of sin is too small a task for the grace of the transcendent God given in this sacrament. The purpose of this sacrament, as indeed is the purpose of all sacraments, is to lead the soul to a greater union with God. To transform the soul so that it can enter into the very life of God. In the process of doing this, the human person is healed and sin is rooted out. Grace will not only heal our broken nature and restore our original innocence, but is necessary for us to achieve our final destiny – complete union with God: Deification. As the author of *The Cloud of Unknowing* puts it,

He who patiently abides in this darkness will be comforted and again feel a confidence about his destiny, for gradually he will see his past sins healed by grace.[94]

---

94   *The Cloud of Unknowing and the Book of Privy Counselling.* William Johnston Trans. Image Books. New York, 1996,Ch69.

In the process of transforming each person, the grace of reconciliation will give a true knowledge of self and of God. The ultimate purpose of this grace is such a full union with God that it leads to the deification of the soul.

Anointing of the Sick – the Oil of Faith

O Holy Father, Physician of souls and bodies, Who didst send Thine Only-begotten Son, our Lord Jesus Christ, Who healeth every infirmity and delivereth from death: Do Thou heal Thy servant, N., of the bodily and spiritual infirmities which possess him (her), and enliven him (her) through the grace of Thy Christ: Through the prayers of our Most-holy Sovereign Lady, the Theotokos and Ever-Virgin Mary; by the protection of the honorable and bodiless powers of Heaven; by the power of the precious and lifegiving Cross; through the honorable and glorious Prophet, Forerunner and Baptist John; of the holy, glorious and all-praised Apostles; of the holy, glorious and right-victorious martyrs; of our venerable and God-bearing Fathers; of the holy and unmercenary Physicians, Cosmas and Damian, Cyrus and John, Panteleimon and Hermalaeus, Sampson and Diomedes, Photius and Anicetus; of the holy and righteous Ancestors of God Joachim and Anna, and of all the Saints. For Thou art the Fountain of healing, O our God, and unto Thee do we send up glory, together with Thine Only-begotten Son, and Thy Spirit, One in Essence, now and ever, and unto the ages of ages. Amen[95].

As was noted in the last chapter, stories of Christ's healing are a prominent feature of all the gospels and if the Church is to carry on Christ's mission on earth, or, more accurately, to be the continuing presence of Christ in the world, then it would be expected that healing and concern for the sick would play a prominent part in the life of the Church. Indeed it has done so since apostolic times. This concern for the sick can take many forms but it is most profoundly expressed in the sacrament of Holy Unction or Anointing of the Sick. The Sacrament of Anointing does not remove the mystery of human suffering. Yet its celebration gives us a window into the mystery of a loving God. Our loving God raises up the crucified Son to display his victorious wounds, sitting triumphant at the Father's right hand.

In 1965 a silver lamina (a thin plate) was discovered at Thecua, south of Bethlehem, together with four ancient lamps[96]. It was found to be inscribed with a primitive Aramaic script which described an early version of the sacrament of Anointing of the Sick entitled *Oil of Faith*. The lamina has been dated on physical and textural evidence to the latter part of the first century and is clear evidence of the antiquity of this sacrament in the Church. Although it is obviously a product of early Jewish Christianity, rather than Greco-Roman, it has clear connections with the ritual used in the Church today. Importantly, even at this early date, this was a sacrament of the Church, a ritual action for the healing of the sick, in which it was the faith of the Church which was seen as important and not the faith of the subject or the charismatic gifts of the celebrant.

---

95   Prayer of anointing from the Rite of Unction in the Byzantine Church as given in http://www.fatheralexander. org/booklets/english/holy_unction_e.htm#_Toc26230835. father Alexander's website has been used as the source for all the texts given in this chapter and his discussion of the sacrament has also been helpful.
96   1967. The sacrament of the Sick – A First Century Text, *The Clergy Review* pp 56-61.

In this sacrament the sick are brought before Christ present in his Church. They are anointed with sacred oil to bring about both physical and spiritual healing. The use of oil as a symbol of healing is not arbitrary. Oil is used because in the ancient world it was associated with health and healing in everyday life, even now an athlete will have sore muscles massaged with various oils and linaments. It naturally implies softening, making supple, bringing to life that which was stiff and dead. In the Old Testament oil was also a sign of the grace and the Spirit of God. Kings and prophets were anointed and an abundance of oil was seen as a sign of God's blessing, as an archetype of the good things of God.

How very good and pleasant it is when kindred live together in unity! It is like the precious oil on the head, running down upon the beard, on the beard of Aaron, running down over the collar of his robes[97]

Anointing with oil was seen as a sign of God's grace, bringing joy and hope. This same understanding is evident in the Gospels. In Mark we read that when Jesus sent his disciples out on what amounted to a training mission, as well as preaching and casting out demons, they *"anointed with oil many that were sick, and healed them*[98].*"* This anointing of the sick followed conventional practice and was also possibly done in imitation of the actions of Jesus. It was certainly done with his approval. The practice continued in the early Church as can be seen from the Epistle of James:

"Is any sick among you? Let him call for the elders (presbyters) of the Church, and let them pray over him, anointing him with oil in the name of the Lord. And the prayer of faith shall save the sick, and the Lord shall raise him up; and if he has committed sins, they shall be forgiven him[99].*"*

It should be noted that the action referred to here is not a charismatic healing from a particularly gifted individual, as is the case in a modern "Pentecostal" understanding. Rather it is an action of the Church community aimed at both physical and spiritual healing – the two are not separated. The literature of the early Church is replete with references to this sacrament. It is discussed by St. Irenaeus of Lyons, Origen and St. Cyril of Alexandria. Both St. Basil the Great and John Chrysostom, have left prayers for the healing of the infirm which entered later into the Rite of Unction as practiced by the Byzantine Church. It has been formally recognised as a sacrament of the Church since at least the fifth century when Pope Innocent I stipulated that it was one of the "mysteries" of the Church forbidden to those undergoing ecclesiastical penance.

A divergence of practice and understanding occurred between the Latin and

---

97   Psalm 133: 1-3
98   Mark 6:13
99   James 5:14-15

Byzantine Churches from about the 12th century. In the Latin Church the sacrament became increasingly reserved for those who were about to die and came to be known as the sacrament of Extreme Unction (literally; Last Anointing) or the Last Rites. While it was not the intention or teaching of the Church, this had the effect of concentrating the sacrament on spiritual healing and downplaying any role it may have in the physical healing of the believer and clouded its association with, and its origin in the healing mission of Jesus. Allied with this was a widespread, popular belief that this sacrament could only be given once, although this was not official Church teaching. The Byzantine Church maintained the original practice of the Church in that the sacrament could be given to all who are seriously ill and could be given as many times as it was needed. The Second Vatican Council moved to resolve this divergence and align the Latin Church with ancient practice. It corrected some of the erroneous understandings that had grown in the Latin Church and restored the understanding and practice of the early Church as outlined in the Epistle of St. James. It emphasized that the proper rite for the dying was the *Viaticum*[100] and that the anointing of the sick was a sacrament of healing for those who were seriously ill[101].

There are still marked differences between the Latin and Byzantine Churches in the liturgical celebration of this sacrament but there are now few theological differences. The rite in the Byzantine Church is long and involved and contains many ancient and beautiful prayers while the rite in the Latin Church is, typically, relatively simple and direct.

In the Latin Rite, the ritual begins with a brief prayer of greeting followed by a blessing of the room and the sick person with holy water. A litany for the sick person and a prayer of sorrow for sin is then said. If the sick person requests it, this may take the form of formal confession and absolution. An appropriate gospel reading follows[102]. The priest then lays hands on the sick person, blesses the oil and anoints the sick person on the forehead and hands saying a prayer such as the one below:

God our healer, in this time of sickness you have come to bless N. with your grace. Restore him/her to health and strength, make him/her joyful in spirit, and ready to embrace your will. Grant this through Christ our Lord.

The Our Father is then said and communion is normally given before the final blessing. The ritual may be condensed in emergency situations. This form of the ritual is designed as a private service at the bedside of the sick although it can take a communal form celebrated in a Church. In this case it is often combined with the

---

100 Literally "food for the journey" – a final communion.
101 *Constitution on the Sacred Liturgy*, #21, in Flannery, A (1981) *Vatican II: Conciliar and Post Conciliar Documents*, Veritas, Dublin.
102 Normally either Matthew 11:25-30, Mark 2:1-12 or Luke 7:19-23

celebration of the Eucharist.

In the Latin Rite only one priest is required while, as we shall see below, the full Byzantine celebration requires seven priests. This difference may just be a product of the more practical mindset of the Latin Church, but it may also reflect the difference in emphasis in the understanding of the role of the priest that was noted earlier in our discussion of the sacrament of Penance. In the Latin Church the priest, as an ordained minister of the Church, stands as a physical representative of Christ, stands *in persona Christi*, and hence only one priest is required. In the Byzantine Church the priests stand as representatives of the Church, which is Christ still present in the world. The role of the priest is to bring the sick person into the presence of Christ who heals in and through his Church and the Church is better represented by a group.

The full celebration of the Byzantine Rite requires seven priests and is really designed to be celebrated in a Church, although it is often celebrated by the sick person's bedside and may be modified or even abbreviated according to pastoral need. The rite starts with the use of incense to sanctify the place and those attending. After the opening prayer a psalm is read followed by prayers asking for God's mercy. A second psalm is read and is followed by a series of nine sung prayers which recall the story of salvation and ask for healing. The oil is then blessed with the following prayer:

O Lord Who, through Thy mercies and compassions, healest the disorders of our souls and bodies: Do Thou Thyself, O Master, sanctify this Oil, that it may be effectual unto them that are anointed with it for healing, and for the relief of every passion, of defilement of flesh and spirit, and of every ill; and that thereby may be glorified Thy most-holy Name: of the Father, and of the Son, and of the Holy Spirit, now and ever, and unto the ages of ages. Amen.

This prayer is said quietly by all the priests and is accompanied by a series of sung prayers (troparia). There follows a series of seven anointings, each given by a different priest. At each anointing there is a reading from one of the epistles followed by a Gospel reading and a long prayer specific for each anointing. An example of these prayers is given below:

O Good Lord and the Lover of Mankind, deeply-compassionate and greatly-merciful, plentiful in mercy and rich in good things, O Father of compassions and God of every consolation, Who hast given us strength through Thy holy Apostles to heal the sicknesses of the people with oil and prayer: Do Thou Thyself confirm this Oil for the healing of them that are anointed with it, for the alleviation of every sickness and every wound, and for deliverance from evils for them that await salvation from Thee. Yea, O Master, Lord our God, we beseech Thee, O All-powerful One, to save us all and to sanctify us, O Thou Who alone art the Physician of souls and bodies. O Thou that healest every sickness, do Thou heal Thy servant, N.. Raise him (her) from the bed of suffering through the mercies of Thy goodness; visit him (her) with Thy mercies and compassions; cast out of him (her) every sickness and weakness, that, being raised up by Thy mighty hand, he (she) may serve Thee with all thanksgiving; and that we who now are sharing in Thine ineffable love for man, may sing praises and glorify Thee Who doest things great and wonderful, both glorious and excellent. For Thine it is to have mercy and to save us, O our God, and unto The do we send up glory: to the Father, and to the Son, and to the Holy Spirit, now and ever, and unto the ages of ages[103].

Each priest then anoints the sick person quietly saying the prayer given at the start of this chapter. It is clear from the form of this prayer that it is the whole community of the Church, both past and present, which is being called upon to pray for the sick. Each of the seven anointings develops a different aspect of the love and mercy of God and how this has been expressed in history. It is important to note that the need for forgiveness is given at least as much weight as the need for healing or, to put it another way, the need for spiritual and physical healing is not separated. They were connected during Jesus' mission on earth and they are connected here in the sacrament. This is emphasized in the final prayer which is said by the first priest, while the other six lay the opened book of the gospels text down on the sick person's head.

O Holy King, Deeply-compassionate and Greatly-merciful Lord Jesus Christ, Son and Word of the Living God, Who desirest not the death of a sinner, but that he should turn back and live: I lay not my sinful hand upon the head of him (her) that comes to Thee in sins and asks of Thee, through us, for remission of sins, but through Thy hand, mighty and powerful, which is in this, Thy Holy Gospel which my fellow ministers hold upon the head of Thy servant, N., and I pray with them and entreat Thy merciful love for mankind which remembers not evil, O God, our Saviour, Who, through Thy Prophet Nathan, didst grant remission of his iniquities unto the repentant David, and didst accept the prayer of repentance of Manasseh. And do Thou Thyself, in Thy customary love for mankind, accept Thy servant, N., who repents of his (her) own sins, overlooking his (her) transgressions. For Thou art our God, Who hast given command to forgive even seventy time seven them that have fallen into sins. For as is Thy majesty, so also is Thy mercy, and unto Thee are due all glory, honour and worship, now and ever, and unto the ages of ages. Amen.

The service is then completed with further sung prayers, which ask God for mercy and call upon the Holy Spirit and Our Lady, and a blessing of dismissal.

---

103   Priest's prayer from the fourth anointing.

It is obviously difficult in a practical sense to get the required seven priests together to celebrate this ritual in its fullness and yet the pastoral need for this sacrament may be urgent and unexpected. Different Churches have responded to this pastoral need in different ways. In the Russian Orthodox Church the sacrament may be given by one priest, but he will pray all seven prayers and give all seven anointings. In other Churches an abbreviated form of the service is used with one priest, one set of prayers and only one anointing. This abbreviated ritual is, in fact, similar in structure to the Latin ritual although there are still differences in style – incense is used instead of Holy Water and the Byzantine prayers are longer and more complicated in their language. However, following the reforms of Vatican II, the normal, day to day pastoral practice of the sacrament of Anointing of the Sick may be far more similar in the Latin and Byzantine Churches than would at first be imagined.

Marriage – The Crowning of Creation

In Your indescribable graciousness and great goodness You came to Cana in Galilee, and blessed the marriage which took place there. Thus You made it clear that it is Your will that there should be lawful marriage and from it the procreation of children. Now, Most Holy Master, hear the supplication of us, Your servants. As You were there, so also be here with Your invisible presence; and bless this marriage, granting to Your servants N. and N. a peaceful and long life, matrimonial chastity, mutual love in the bond of peace, a long-lived posterity, happiness in their children, and the unfading crown of glory. Keep their married life above reproach, and grant them to see their childrens' children; give them dew from heaven and the fruitfulness of the earth; provide them with an abundance of temporal good things, that they in turn may share their abundance with those in need; and grant to everyone here present with them all that is necessary for salvation.[104]

Marriage is unique among the sacraments of the Church in that it existed as a social institution in much the same form and with much the same function prior to the emergence of the Christian Church. All of the sacraments take pre-existing elements and sanctify them. However, while Baptism may take water and washing as its basis, it is not washing in the normal sense; and while the Eucharist may be thought of a sacred meal, one does not go to communion because of physical hunger. Yet marriage as a faithful, public bond between a man and a woman, to form a family and for the creation and protection of children, was known long before the Christian era. Even concepts such as monogamy and marital fidelity are very ancient. In marriage, the sacrament seems to have already existed, waiting for the incarnation of Christ to fill it with grace and transcendent meaning. This is why Paul considers that a pagan marriage remains valid even after one of the spouses has become a Christian. Indeed, the pagan marriage is seen not only to remain valid, but now to be filled with the grace of Christ to such an extent that the pagan member of the marriage may be saved by the faith of the Christian member.

An elderly parishioner ventured the opinion that, "Marriage was instituted by God in the Garden of Eden and blessed by Christ at the marriage feast at Cana. What more is there to say?". In its simplicity this statement holds a great truth. Most of the sacraments have their origins in the love and grace of God's action of redemption. Marriage has its origins in the love and grace of God's action of creation. Marriage is a part of what humanity was created to be: *Then the Lord God said, "It is not good that the man should be alone; I will make him a helper fit for him.[105]*

The other sacraments have their origins in the life and mission of Christ and can be seen as a continuation of that mission through the ministry of the Church. Marriage

---

104   From Byzantine Catholic marriage rite
105   Genesis 2: 18

has its origins in creation itself and can be seen as a continuation of the charge given to humanity at the very beginning of their creation.

So God created man in his own image, in the image of God he created him; male and female he created them. And God blessed them, and God said to them, "Be fruitful and multiply, and fill the earth and subdue it; and have dominion over the fish of the sea and over the birds of the air and over every living thing that moves upon the earth."[106]

Like all things, of course, marriage was damaged and corrupted by the fall and needed to be redeemed by the love and grace of God in Christ. However, marriage remains tied to creation in a particular way. The other sacraments were created by Christ in his mission and in his Church, but marriage, like all of creation, already existed and was redeemed by Christ and filled with His grace. It is notable that when Jesus is called upon to discuss marriage[107], he does not do so by referring to rabbinical law, nor to any of the stories of marriage in the Old Testament. Instead, He goes back to the very beginning and refers to a passage from Genesis. This passage is, therefore, essential to a proper understanding of marriage.

Then the man said, "This at last is bone of my bones and flesh of my flesh; she shall be called Woman, because she was taken out of Man." Therefore a man leaves his father and his mother and cleaves to his wife, and they become one flesh. And the man and his wife were both naked, and were not ashamed.[108]

This does not mean that Marriage is somehow separate from the story of salvation. Rather, it is deeply a part of it. The sacramentality of marriage shows that the salvation of Christ reaches to the very core of our being, to every corner of what it is to be human. This understanding of marriage as fundamental to human existence and society, this link between marriage and creation, and Christian marriage's transformation by the Holy Spirit to a new and transcendent reality, is the key to a deeper appreciation of a sacrament which is so much abused in modern western society. It is also the key to a proper understanding of sex, which our modern society has also turned into a commodity, but which the Christian Church, both east and west, sees as a sacred sharing in the creative energy of God.

In the early centuries of the Church there was no distinct ritual for marriage[109]. A Christian couple would go and make the marriage agreement according to Roman civil law and then attend Eucharist. They may have asked for a blessing from the priest, although there is no evidence of a distinct marriage blessing prior to the fourth century. It was the first communion together as a couple which was

---

106 Genesis 1: 27,28
107 Matthew 19; Mark 10;
108 Genesis 2: 23-25
109 Many of the facts in this section are taken from the history given in Meyendorff, J. 1975, *Marriage: An Orthodox Perspective*, St. Vladimir's Seminary Press. The interpretation given to these events, however, are my own.

considered to be the sacramental symbol of the marriage. It was only slowly that a distinct and definitive marriage ritual developed. As late as the ninth century, the Patriarch Photius wrote that: *"Marriage is an alliance between husband and wife and their union for their entire life; it is accomplished by a blessing, or by a crowning, or by an agreement.*[110]*"* The point here is that there were still three different ways in which a Christian marriage could be conducted.

The Christian sacrament of marriage became increasingly involved with the Roman secular institution of marriage after Christianity was recognised by the Emperor Constantine. The development of the Christian marriage ritual was thus effected when the Roman Empire split into its Eastern and Western components. In the west, the break down of civil society meant that the Church assumed much of the civil responsibility for marriage and could largely dictate its form. The western Church preserved the blessing and first communion together as the nuptial ritual and simply incorporated the public promises which formed the Roman civil practice. In the east, the marriage ritual increasingly became a matter of imperial edict and was separated from the Eucharist to preserve the sacredness of the Eucharistic celebration. The current form of Marriage ritual, the crowning, seems to have come to the Church from Armenia and was first mandated by the Emperor Leo VI (+912) and then confirmed and made universal by the Emperor Alexis I Comnenos (1081 – 1118). This separate history has profoundly effected the understanding each Church has of marriage.

There is relatively little written about the theology of marriage in the Byzantine Church, especially if you compare it to the extensive literature in the Latin Church. It is fair to say that this is an area where the distinctive understanding of the Byzantine Church, as opposed to the common understanding which she shares with the Latin Church, remains implicit in Church practice rather than being fully expressed in explicit theology. This poses a problem for an outsider who wishes to have a deeper understanding than that which can be gained from descriptions of ritual practice. Where written theology is absent, two keys remain to the faith of the Byzantine Church: the liturgy and the icon. The most important icon relating to marriage is that of the Wedding Feast at Cana during which Christ blessed the human bonds of marriage and conferred on them a sacramental character. This incident at the beginning of Christ's ministry[111] is seen as pivotal by both Churches in any understanding of marriage. Christ's actions at Cana show that he approves and blesses the human bonds of marriage, and more than that, fills them with His life and grace so that they become much more than they were before – *"..you have saved the best wine till last."* The fact that John places this incident at the beginning of Christ's ministry not only emphasizes the importance of marriage but makes it a kind of introduction to what is to follow. Christ's mission on Earth is a call to all

110 quoted in Meyendorff, J. 1975, *Marriage: An Orthodox Perspective*, St. Vladimir's Seminary Press.
111 John 2:1-12

of humanity to the wedding feast of the Apocalyptic Lamb – a theme which recurs many times in the Gospels. A meditation on this icon will, hopefully, allow us to develop an appreciation of the Byzantine Church's distinctive understanding of marriage.

The first thing to notice about the icon of the Wedding Feast at Cana is that it is literally a feast. The table occupies the central position in the icon and it is loaded with food and drink. On the table there is meat, poultry, fish, bread, fruit and vegetables. In short, all of the fruits of the Earth, all the good things of creation, are laid out before the bride. This clearly establishes the link between marriage and creation, between marriage and the abundance of creation - *Be fruitful and multiply, and fill the earth.* The central position of this laden table indicates that this relationship between marriage and creation is fundamental to any proper understanding of marriage. Marriage is about celebrating all the good things in life, which God in His love has given us. It is about the abundant love of God for all His creation - *"give them dew from heaven and the fruitfulness of the earth; provide them with an abundance of temporal good things..." (Byzantine Marriage Service)*

At the head of this table of nature's abundance, and occupying the central position in the icon, is the figure of the bride, crowned as in the Byzantine wedding ceremony.

Traditional Icon of the Wedding Feast at Cana

There is a startling similarity between the figure of the bride shown here at the start of Christ's ministry, and the figure of "old man Cosmos" in the icon of Pentecost, at the start of the mission of the Church. Old man Cosmos represented the world held in the bondage of sin. Here, the bride represents the other side of that coin, she is nature, good and graced by its creation by God and yet lacking something vital. The table is laden, but they have no wine and the feast is turning sour, as the bowed head of the servant in the upper left of the icon shows. In modern, western terms we might consider the bride to represent "Mother Nature" but it would be more traditional, and more accurate, to consider the bride as a symbol of Sophia. Sophia is a concept which is largely unfamiliar to the west but which plays an important role in Eastern Theology. It was perhaps best described by the Russian philosopher and theologian Pavel Florensky. Florensky saw creation as "one living being praying to its creator and Father." This one, living being he called Sophia – the divine wisdom. Sophia is in creation from its first being and yet is in the process of becoming. Sophia is the spiritual beauty of creation, the incorruptible, first-created beauty of creation and the glory of creation struggling to be born. Here Sophia as the bride connects human marriage with this great act of becoming, of giving birth. In marriage, humanity is opened to the full, awesome creativity of life.

Yet there is something lacking. They have no wine and Mary stands apart from the table, although she is clearly also a guest at the feast, and presents the need of the wedding party, the need of creation, to Christ. Here Mary is the embodiment of the Church acting in a priestly role and she brings the needs of the world to God and asks for His mercy and compassion. In marriage it is the Church which presents the couple to Christ in their most intimate need and longing, and asks for the grace of his Spirit to bless them and to fill their need. It is then that the miraculous happens and the water is changed into wine. The same thing happens in Christian marriage. A couple's love for each other is always contingent and flavoured with self-love in the natural order, as all things of this world are. However, when the Church presents the couple to God, the natural love and relationship which the couple have had up until now, which was good in itself but limited, is transformed into some thing far greater. It is infused with the Spirit of God and transcends its natural human character to become an expression, a manifestation, of the divine love. The water of human *eros* becomes the wine of divine *agape*.

The role of the Church in marriage is to bring the couple before Christ who bestows this miraculous blessing upon them. Just as Mary is central to the story of the marriage feast at Cana, so the Church is central to each Christian marriage. Christian, sacramental marriage is a Church affair. Indeed it is here that the Church is reborn with the new family forming a new Christian community which shares in all the qualities of the Church – "a community of grace and prayer, a school of human virtues and Christian charity"[112]. This is called the 'little Church' in Orthodox Church literature[113] or the 'domestic Church' in the literature of the Roman Catholic Church[114]. In this Christian community the parents play a priestly role, offering themselves and their children to Christ and instructing their children in the practice of the Christian faith.

One other notable feature of the icon of the wedding feast of Cana is that the bride is the only one crowned. Although the male figure sitting to the left of her is presumably the groom, he wears no crown. This is to emphasis another relationship, that between Christ and his creation, symbolized in the bride. This is what Paul meant when he said in his letter to the Ephesians:

As the Church is subject to Christ, so let wives also be subject in everything to their husbands. Husbands, love your wives, as Christ loved the Church and gave himself up for her, ...He who loves his wife loves himself. For no man ever hates his own flesh, but nourishes and cherishes it, as Christ does the Church, because we are members of his body. "For this reason a man shall leave his father and mother and be joined to his wife, and the two shall become one flesh." This mystery is a profound one, and I am saying that it refers to Christ and the Church.[115]

Every wedding is itself a symbol and foretaste of the great wedding feast where Christ will be joined to his bride, the Church and, through the Church, to all of the created order. The love of man and woman is itself a sacrament of the love of Christ and the Church. The two become one in a life of mutual love and mutual subjection to each other in Christ just as Christ gives himself to and for His Church and the Church bows down before Him. There is a sense in which at every wedding it is Christ who presides and Christ who is the bridegroom. Every wedding is a call to the eternal wedding feast of the Lamb.

Marriage thus has an intrinsically Eucharistic character. The couple offer themselves up to each other, give themselves to each other and are received and blessed by God in unity just as in the Eucharist the Church offers up all of creation. Christ gives himself totally and the Church enters into a blessed union with Christ in which she is brought into the love of the Father and the life of the Spirit. Marriage and the Eucharist have been joined in the understanding of the Church since the very earliest days.

In the Byzantine Church the actual marriage ceremony is now separated from the celebration of the Eucharist. This was done when the Church took over the imperial administration of marriage and it was necessary to preserve the sacredness of the

112 The Catechism of the Catholic Church, 1666, St Paul's Press, Homebush, NSW.
113 Stavropoulos, A.M. 1979, The Understanding of Marriage in the Orthodox Church. *One in Christ* Vol. XV, No. 1, pp57-63.
114 Lumen Gentium #11, in Flannery, A (1981) *Vatican II: Conciliar and Post Conciliar Documents*, Veritas, Dublin.
115 Ephesians 5: 24-32

Eucharistic celebration from the intrusion of imperial processes, rights and edicts. This is a great pity since it obscures the connection between marriage and the Pascal feast of the Lamb. Even though some Orthodox theologians have claimed that the form of the ritual still maintains a Eucharistic connection[116], others have called for the ritual to include a Eucharistic celebration so that this connection is made clear[117]. The current Byzantine marriage ritual is split into two distinct parts: the exchange of rings, or the betrothal, and the crowning.

The first part of the ritual is the betrothal or the exchange of rings. It is conducted in the vestibule of the Church, the part of the Church closest to the outside world. This is the equivalent of the old Roman civil marriage and prior the Council of Trent a similar ritual existed in many parts of the Latin Church, with the couple being greeted at the door of the Church by the priest. In this part of the ritual the rings are blessed by the priest and then placed on each right hand – the hand used for making promises and oaths and the hand used to make the sign of the cross. In this part of the service the Church prays for the union of the couple which has begun in the world but which is now destined to eschatological union in Christ.

O Lord our God, Who accompanied the servant of the patriarch Abraham to Mesopotamia, when he was sent to espouse a wife for his lord Isaac, and did reveal to him a sign by the drawing of water to betroth Rebecca; do You Yourself bless the betrothal of these Your servants (Name) and (Name) and confirm the word that has been spoken by them; for You, O Lord, from the beginning have created male and female, and by You is a woman joined to a man for assistance and for the continuation of the human race. Therefore, O Lord God, Who have sent forth Your truth to Your inheritance and Your promise to Your servants, our fathers, who were Your elect, do You give regard unto this Your servant (Name) and Your servant (Name), and seal their betrothal in faith, in oneness of mind, in truth and in love. ...Yea, by the word of Your truth were the Heavens established and the earth set upon her sure foundations; and the right hands of Your servants shall be blessed by Your mighty word, and by Your uplifted arm. Wherefore, O Sovereign Lord, do You Yourself bless this putting on of rings with Your heavenly benediction; and may Your Angel go before them all the days of their life, for You are He that blesses and sanctifies all things, and to You do we send up Glory: to the Father, and to the Son, and to the Holy Spirit, both now and ever, and to the ages of ages.[118]

The couple then process into the Church where they state their free intention to marry and that there is no impediment to them doing so. They are then presented with lighted candles, a symbol of the light of Christ which will guide them through life, which they hold throughout the rest of the service.

---

116 Charalambidis, S. 1979. Marriage in the Orthodox Church, *One in Christ*, Vol. XV No.3, pp204-223.
117 Meyendorff, J. 1975, *Marriage: An Orthodox Perspective*, St. Vladimir's Seminary Press.
118 Extract from the final prayer of the betrothal service.

After they have stated their intention and prayers have been offered for them, the groom and bride are crowned by the priest "In the Name of the Father and of the Son and of the Holy Spirit". The crowns are symbols of the both the couple's share in the kingship of Christ and of the witness, the martyrdom, involved in the life of mutual self-giving to which the couple are now committed. Just as the martyrs gave witness to Christ with their lives and received the crown of glory, so the common life of the bride and groom is to bear witness to the presence of Christ in their lives and in the world.

Holy God, Who fashioned man from the dust, and from his rib fashioned woman, and joined her to him as a helpmate for him, for it was seemly unto Your Majesty for man not to be alone upon the earth, do You Yourself, O Sovereign Lord, stretch forth Your hand from Your holy dwelling place, and join together this Your servant (Name) and Your servant (Name), for by You is a wife joined to her husband. Join them together in oneness of mind; crown them with wedlock into one flesh; grant to them the fruit of the womb, and the gain of well favored children, for Yours is the dominion, and Yours is the Kingdom, and the Power, and the Glory: of the Father, and of the Son, and of the Holy Spirit, both now and ever, and to the ages of ages[119].

The scriptures are then read, the couple drink blessed wine from a common cup as a sign of their union, and they process around the central table three times as a symbol of their progression through life together – this is called the Dance of Isiah. The crowns are then removed and the couple is presented to the congregation.

The Father, the Son, and the Holy Spirit; the All-Holy, Consubstantial and Life-creating Trinity; One Godhead and Kingdom; bless (+) you; grant to you long life, well-favored children, progress in life and in Faith; replenish you with all the good things of the earth, and count you worthy of the promised blessings, through the intercessions of the holy Theotokos, and of all the Saints[120].

The Byzantine Church believes that marriage is forever; that it is a mystery transcending time and space in which the couple participate in and are incorporated into the life of the Triune God. This why the marriage ceremony in the Orthodox Church includes no reference to "until death do us part" and why there are restrictions on the number of times a widow or widower can be married. The same restrictions apply here as in divorce – an Orthodox Christian may be married a total of three times, whatever the circumstances. Death is not seen as parting the married couple, their union continues within the communion of saints. Some Orthodox theologians believe that since the Catholic Church places no restriction on sacramental re-marriage after the death of a spouse, the Catholic Church teaches that marriage ends at death and that this is a point of difference between the two

119   Priest's prayer at the crowning.
120   Final blessing of the couple.

Churches. However, while this may be accepted by some Catholic theologians, it has never been taught definitively by the Church and other theological opinions, more in accord with the Orthodox understanding, also have strong support within the Catholic Church. Consider the following extract from a sermon given by Fr Cantalamessa, the Pontifical Household Preacher:

...marriage does not come to a complete end at death but is transfigured, spiritualized, freed from the limits that mark life on earth, as also the ties between parents and children or between friends will not be forgotten. In a preface for the dead the liturgy proclaims: "Life is transformed, not taken away." Even marriage, which is part of life, will be transfigured, not nullified[121].

If marriage lasts forever, how is it then that an Orthodox Christian can get divorced and still be married a second time, and even a third time, in the Church? Fundamentally this is a reluctant concession which arises from pastoral concern and from the recognition that in marriage we are dealing with the mystery of the human person – the weak, sinful and needy human person. However, marriage after divorce is not considered the same as the first marriage. The second marriage is seen to be the result of weakness and sin and it has a penitential character. The great, overflowing joy of the first marriage ceremony is no longer evident.

Under any circumstances, an Orthodox Christian can only be married three times. After that, no further marriage within the Church is possible. This restriction has its origin in the political ambition of an Emperor who, for reasons of diplomacy, wanted to be married a fourth time. The Patriarch was troubled and wrote to the pope asking if this was permissible. The Pope replied that a fourth marriage was impossible and so it has stayed. It is intriguing to consider what might have happened if the Patriarch had written to the Pope earlier.

In the Orthodox Church, remarriage after divorce is possible because in the Byzantine understanding it is the Church, as Christ present on earth, which marries the couple. The proper minister of the sacrament is the priest who confers the sacrament on the couple. Since the Church confers the sacrament, the Church has the authority to declare the marriage void. This is a very different understanding of the sacrament to that of the Latin Church.

In the western Church it is the couple who are the ministers of the sacrament. The Church, represented by the priest or deacon, blesses and receives their action, joining their union to the union of Christ and the Church, but it is the free consent of the couple which forms the material of the sacrament and this consent is finally sealed by the marriage act itself. This is why, prior to the Council of Trent, in many western countries the final nuptial blessing was given in the bed chamber[122].

---

121 Father Cantalamessa on Marriage in Heaven, http://www.catholic.org/, 11/11/2006 - 6:00 AM PST
122 *The Church at Prayer,* A.G. Martimort (Ed.) Vol. III *The Sacraments,* Chapter VI *Marriage* by J. Evenou,

Sex between a husband and wife is thus a sacramental action through which God gives them the grace to live their lives together and blesses them with children. Some Orthodox writers have considered that the western view of marriage to be that of a legal contract[123]. This is a serious misunderstanding. If marriage were a legal contract then it could, presumably, be dissolved by mutual consent. In the Latin Church's understanding, however, marriage consists of a mystical union at an ontological level. The two have become one flesh and a new creature is born, a new Church, a new bride for Christ. It is because of this that the Catholic Church does not consider that it has the authority to admit remarriage after divorce. While it might be necessary in the civil arena, the Catholic Church considers sacramental divorce to be simply impossible. Catholics of the Byzantine rite are also bound by this discipline.

Here we have perhaps a reversal of the normal outlooks of the two Churches, Latin and Byzantine, with the Latin Church developing a deep, mystical understanding of the sacrament while the Orthodox understanding, to many Roman Catholics, seems too closely tied to administration and issues of Church authority. The insistence that it has no authority to marry someone after divorce, however, leaves the Catholic Church with a deep and persistent pastoral problem. How do you care not only for the people whose marriage has ended, but those whose marriage was clearly something of a sham to begin with? A partial answer is provided by the process of annulment. Since the free consent of the couple is the key material of the sacrament, if this were lacking in any way, either through some from of coercion or individual impairment, then the sacrament can not take place. Thus, while the marriage exists physically and legally, the sacramental union can not have been formed. In such a case, the Catholic Church recognizes that there was no sacramental marriage, even if the proper form was followed, and the couple are free to remarry. However, all Christian marriage is a Church affair. It is as members of the Church that the couple marry each other and their action is joined, indeed is part of, the prayer of the whole Church. Church recognition of the fact of the nullity of the sacramental marriage is thus necessary for the members to play a full role in the ongoing life of the Church. This does, however, lead to the faintly ridiculous situation where canon lawyers are asked to sit down and decide the deepest motivations of the human heart and even what those motivations may have been many years ago.

There is an irony here in that by taking a deeply mystical approach to the sacrament, the Catholic Church finds itself entangled in a bureaucratic legal process while the Orthodox Church, by taking a more administrative approach, finds itself relatively free of such problems.

No discussion of the sacrament of marriage would be complete without a

---

Geoffrey Chapman, London, 1987.
123 Meyendorff, J. 1975, *Marriage: An Orthodox Perspective*, St. Vladimir's Seminary Press.

discussion of sex, since the sexual act is a fundamental part of marriage. Our modern society tends to separate sex and marriage - to treat sex as a commodity or as an entertainment. Sometimes, normally in response to the needs of marketing, sex is portrayed as "naughty" with all the glamour of sin attached to it. Such views are profoundly at odds with a proper Christian understanding of sex. If marriage is a sacrament, then sex between a husband and wife is sacred, a source of grace and holiness. This understanding has not always been evident in the teachings of the Church. Early Christian writings had a tendency to see sex as a kind of split in creation, an inevitable consequence of man's mixed nature of flesh and spirit. This Neo-platonist and Gnostic view infiltrated the thought of some of the greatest Church Fathers and colluded with a hatred of sex and of women, to cast out love from the world, portraying it as enticing lust, alluring falsehood, sweet poison or simply as 'paganism'.124 As Lampert points out, this infiltration has had disastrous consequences, because it

...killed the great religious dream of the holiness of sex and of love, and of life as the feast of love. Sex was driven into the prison of bourgeois family existence and domesticity, where it was 'tolerated'; or else it was or is dragging on an irreligious life in night-clubs and similar institutions-a fatal counterpoise of marriage and the family conceived as mere matrimonial transactions. Sexual love found itself outside religion, unsanctified, abandoned to the whims of fate or...of the devil."125

This was a view later expressed independently by Pope Benedict XVI in his first encyclical – *Deus charitas est*. In response to this history, Lampert claims that the creation of woman is the very acknowledgment of the reality of sex as the fulfillment of creation; that sex is a transcendent reality, and that *'sexual life has a transcendent significance,* while *'the union of the sexes in love is a witness to the fullness of being and life eternal.'* It is a true tragedy that the holiness of sexual love has been so blasphemed: on the one hand by cold dualism, detesting the flesh as a source of defilement, and on the other, by an amoral monism which sees the flesh as the theatre of mere animal activity. Both are blind to *'the mystery and sacrament of holy flesh',* as the *'way of ascent into the heavens and the grace of the Holy Spirit descending on it'126*

Over the course of the 20th century the Christian Church has gradually thrown away its neo-platonic and Gnostic baggage and awoken to the unity of all love and to the sacredness of married, sexual love. At a time when the world separates sex from procreation, from marriage, from faithfulness and even from the most superficial concept of love, the Church has rediscovered its own heritage and understands

---

124 *Divine Realm*, 93.
125 *Divine Realm*, 94.
126 *Divine Realm*, 97.

anew the sacred, transcendent nature of sexual love. Love, including sexual love, was the chosen topic of Pope Benedict XVI's first encyclical – *Deus caritas est.* This is what he has to say on the unity of eros and agape.

Yet eros and agape—ascending love and descending love—can never be completely separated. The more the two find a proper unity in the one reality of love, the more the true nature of love in general is realized. Even if eros is at first mainly covetous and ascending, a fascination for the great promise of happiness, in drawing near to the other, it is less and less concerned with itself, increasingly seeks the happiness of the other, is concerned more and more with the beloved, bestows itself and wants to "be there for" the other. The element of agape thus enters into this love, for otherwise eros is impoverished and even loses its own nature. On the other hand, man cannot live by oblative, descending love alone. He cannot always give, he must also receive. Anyone who wishes to give love must also receive love as a gift.

Holy Orders – An Icon of Christ

From the time of the Exodus from Egypt and the establishment of the covenant between God and the people of Israel, until the final destruction of the temple by Roman troops in 70AD, the temple priesthood played a central role in the life of the Jewish people. Indeed, temple observance was a prime constituent of Jewish identity. It was the ritual centre that acted to unify the many factions that comprised the Jewish nation, particularly for those Jews living in their homeland. So important was the priesthood to the Jews that significant portions of the books of Leviticus, Numbers and Deuteronomy are given over to the formation, the duties, and even the dress of the priesthood. It might be thought then that this priesthood would be the basis or the model for the priesthood in the new Christian Church with its Jewish origins and strong Jewish heritage. The new priesthood might even have been expected to be seen as a reformed continuation of the old priesthood. However, this is not so and St. Paul specifically rejects any such suggestion[127]. The new Christian priesthood was based on the priesthood of Christ, and was of the order of Melchisidek[128].

Melchisidek is the mysterious figure described in Genesis as a king of Salem and a priest of the Most High God. After a raid in which Abram had rescued his nephew Lot, Melchisidek offered a sacrifice for Abram, an offering of bread and wine. He blessed him in the name of the Most High God. This was just prior the God's promise to Abram to make him a father of a great nation. This event is seen as significant for Christianity, not just because of the obvious symbolism of the bread and wine, but because in the Psalms the messiah, the Christ, is to be given an eternal priesthood of the order of Melchisidek[129]. The name Melchisidek means "king of righteousness", a title later given to the messiah and seen by Christians as referring to Christ.

The key thing about the Melchisidek reference is that this is not the Levitical or Aaronic priesthood of the Jewish law. Jewish priesthood was an hereditary priesthood, handed down from father to son, and because Jesus was of the line of David and not from one of the priestly families, he could never be a part of that hereditary priesthood. The Jewish priesthood offered sacrifices to God on behalf of the people so that God might grant them blessings and the forgiveness of their sins. In this sense, this was a priesthood similar to that of their pagan neighbors. Where they differed, of course, was in their understanding of the nature of God. They knew that there was only one God who was a loving God concerned with the welfare of His people. The sacrifices were not payments as such, except as metaphor, rather

---

127 Hebrews 8:13
128 Hebrews 8:13
129 Psalm 110:4

they were a symbol of the people's repentance and sorrow: a sacramental action.

Wherever you have a system of hereditary privilege, however, there is the danger of corruption and one of the themes of the gospels is the corruption of the Jewish priesthood and the need for it to be replaced. This is first shown in the figure of John the Baptist, who was himself of a priestly family, and could have claimed his place in the temple. He chose, however, to reject the corruption of the old religious system and lived as an ascetic, preaching a new sacramental action of repentance: baptism. The change was significant. In the old temple sacrifices the priest offered gifts to God in appeasement for sin or in the hope of blessing. In baptism you offer nothing but your sorrow, and you are given the gift of forgiveness by God. The action is now God's action and John prophesized that the time will come when God will fill this action with the fire of His own Spirit: when the symbol will take on a new divine reality. The baptism of Christ by John is thus considered very important in the Byzantine Church. In this incident John, a righteous member of the old priesthood, recognizes in Christ a new order of priesthood far greater than his own. The best of the old recognizes and gives way to the new. That is why in the icon of Christ's baptism there is an imp with an axe about to cut down a tree. The old way is passing and a new priesthood is being established[130].

The new priesthood is established and exists in the person of Christ whose sacrifice on Calvary was an eternal sacrifice which forever changed the relationship between God and man. On Calvary God overcame the limited and wholly inadequate nature of human sin offerings by offering His own self. The divine person, the incarnate word of God, suffered death and all of reality was shaken to its core. On the cross, all the sin and evil of the world was forever overcome by the triumph of God's love. This priestly act is the fountainhead of all Christian priesthood.

Christ is the one eternal high priest who in his own person overcomes the contingent, limited and symbolic nature of earlier offerings. In his one eternal sacrifice Christ has brought the whole of creation, transformed and divinized by his own incarnation, as an offering to God. The offering is accepted and a new order of being, the Kingdom of God, is established and celebrated in the resurrection. All space and time are now one great Amen in this heavenly liturgy.

All Christian priesthood is an expression of the priesthood of Christ. There is no way, and there is no sense, in which a Christian can exercise any priesthood other than the priesthood of Christ. Indeed, even the actions of the pagan priests only ever had any real meaning because of and through Christ's priesthood. This goes to the core of our own human nature. We are created as a priestly people. We are creation aware of itself and aware of God. It is the deepest expression of our being

---

130 Within forty years of this event the temple had been destroyed and the Jewish priesthood has passed forever into history. The Jewish people had to come to a new understanding of their identity before God and rabbinical Judaism as we currently know it was born.

to offer our world back to God in love. Our offerings on their own are always sin ridden and broken, but joined to the perfect offering of Christ, in whom human nature is perfected, they become glorious. At the end of time the fullness of the Church will be seen to encompass all of creation and the Spirit will present her to Christ as a spotless and beautiful bride. Christ will then escort her to the Father and into the very life of the Holy Trinity.

Consequently, all Christians are called to priesthood by their baptism. This priesthood of the Christian people is not the same as the ordained priesthood. It can not substitute for the ordained priesthood, nor does it make the ordained priesthood unnecessary. However, the priesthood of all Christians is nevertheless very much a reality and not just a pious idea. To fail to recognize the reality of this priesthood is to run the risk of clericalism, where ordained ministers take over the proper functions of the laity and the laity become passive recipients of a sacral service. The priesthood of all Christians is a priesthood of prayer and service which offers up to God everyday life and the secular world in which Christians live. Christians are meant to be Christ in the world, and when they make Christ present, by word or deed, they exercise their priesthood. An artist or poet praising God for the beauty of the world around them, a farmer praying for rain, a doctor or nurse serving Christ in the sick, even the publican serving Christ in the person of the stranger, all of these are exercising their Christian priesthood. In serving Christ incarnate in the needy of the world they become Christ in the world and join in his offering of all of creation to the Father.

This priesthood is most profoundly expressed in marriage where it takes on a sacramental character. The husband and wife dedicate themselves to each other in a mutual self giving and care for and teach their children so that they may in their turn come to know, love and serve God. As was noted previously, for much of the history of the Byzantine Church the exact number of the sacraments was not defined and other modes of Christian life have at times been proposed as formally sacramental. The rituals to enter these modes of life would then have been defined formally as sacraments. Two of these are of particular significance in the culture and history of the Byzantine Church: the entry into religious life, becoming a monk or nun, and the crowning of a king or emperor. However, the tradition of the Church is that, while these are both important roles which do have a broad sacramental character, they are not the equivalent of the great sacraments of the Church which frame and define Christian life.

There are also clerical ranks which are seen to share the same character; blessed Church appointments which are nonetheless not a part of the sacrament of Holy Orders. In the past these were quiet numerous, but they have now been reduced to two: reader and sub-deacon. A similar development has taken place in the Latin Rite Catholic Church which has reduced its non-ordained clerical ranks to those of

Lector and Acolyte. The status of the ancient rank of deaconess is still a matter of dispute in both Churches.

It was previously noted that the priesthood of all Christians cannot substitute or be interchanged with the ordained priesthood conferred by the sacrament of Holy Orders. This is because, even though this ordained priesthood also stems from a participation in the priesthood of Christ, it has a fundamentally different purpose – it is a different thing. When St John Chrysostom wrote his treatise on the priesthood, he linked the purpose of the priesthood to the passage in the gospel of John where the resurrected Christ asks Peter three times if he loves him. Peter answers in the affirmative each time and is told to feed and tend Christ's lambs and sheep[131]. St. John Chrysostom sees the meaning of the passage as follows:

The master asked the disciple if He was loved by him, not in order to get information (how should He who penetrates the hearts of all men?), but in order to teach us how great an interest He takes in the care of these sheep. This being plain, it will likewise be clear that a great and unspeakable reward will be reserved for him whose labours are concerned with these sheep, upon which Christ places such a high value[132].

The key point here is that the ordained priesthood is primarily concerned with the care of God's people. Its mission is to instruct, to guide, to support and to sacramentaly enable the people of God to exercise their priesthood in the world. One of the pope's titles is "the servant of the servants of God". Properly understood, this applies to all bishops, priests and deacons. Authority, respect and position are never to be sought for themselves, but only as a means to serve God's people. Christian leadership is always meant to be an exercise in service.

Preaching and instruction, by both word and example, are clearly a key part of this but it is the sacramental leadership which is the most defining characteristic. An insight can be gained here by looking at those Protestant groups which have largely conflated the ordained priesthood with that of all Christians, making the pastoral leadership simply a job or appointed position. In these groups the sacramental life of the Church has also been greatly diminished. There is a vital connection between the sacrament of Holy Orders and the sacramental life of the Church. It is in the Divine Liturgy that the Priesthood finds its most important role, its true nature and its dignity. As St. John Chrysostom says:

For the priestly office is indeed discharged on earth, but it ranks amongst heavenly ordinances; and very naturally so: for neither man, nor angel, nor archangel, nor any other created power, but the Paraclete Himself, instituted this vocation, and

---

131 John 21:15-17
132 John Chrysostom, *Treatise on the Priesthood*, Book II. Accessed in *Nicene and Post-Nicene Fathers*, Series I, Vol. IX, www.ccel.org/fathers2/NPNF1-09/npnf1-09-07.htm

persuaded men while still abiding in the flesh to represent the ministry of angels…
For when you see the Lord sacrificed, and laid upon the altar, and the priest
standing and praying over the victim, and all the worshipers empurpled with that
precious blood, can you think that you are still amongst men and standing on the
Earth? Are you not, on the contrary, straightaway translated to heaven…?[133]

Priesthood is not just a job, it is not just (or even!) a position of institutional power.
It is a special calling and grace to make manifest Christ, the eternal high priest. A
Christian priest can exercise no priesthood other than the priesthood of Christ. He can
offer no sacrifice other than the sacrifice of Christ. Cut off from Christ he has no sacral
power at all, but in the power of the Spirit it is through him that Christ is made present
to His people and it is through him that God's grace flows to console, to empower and
to sanctify God's people. Just as there is a clericalism in which ordained ministers
take over roles proper to the laity, there is also an anti-clericalism, or laicism, which
sees the laity attempting to perform the duties proper to the ordained ministry. Both
are destructive to the proper life of the Church.

All levels of the ordained ministry (bishops, priests and deacons) are considered in
Byzantine thought as icons of Christ and His Church. In the Byzantine Church an
icon is a sacred image which makes present the divine reality it portrays. Just as
the incarnate Christ is an image of the Father, and makes the Father accessible to
our limited minds and senses, so sacred images make the sacred realities portrayed
in them present and accessible to our limited, mortal senses. Because of early
controversies over the role of sacred images (the iconoclast controversies) which
rocked the Eastern Church, but not the Western Church, the Eastern Church has
a very highly developed theology of the sacred image. This issue was a subject
discussed in the 7th Ecumenical Council (the last ecumenical council of the
undivided Church) held in Nicea in 787. While making a distinction between
worship (due to God alone) and reverence (given to sacred objects and images),
the council reaffirmed the role of icons because:

The more often that they (Jesus and the saints) are seen in artistic representations,
the more we are uplifted by the memory of their prototypes, and brought to a
longing for them;…For the honour which is paid to the image passes on to that
which the image represents, and the one who revers the image revers in it the
person represented[134].

Saying that a bishop, priest or deacon is an icon of Christ and His Church thus has
a more specific meaning in the Eastern Church than it would have in the west. The
ordained ministers make Christ present and accessible to God's people, not through
their appearance or personal characteristics but by virtue of the sacramental grace of

---

133   *Treatise on the Priesthood,* Book III. Accessed in *Nicene and Post-Nicene Fathers,* Series I, Vol. IX,
      www.ccel.org/fathers2/NPNF1-09/npnf1-09-08.htm
134   Seventh Ecuminical Council or the Second Council of Nicea

their ordination. The great reverence offered to priests in many Orthodox countries, which will include kissing the hands of the priest, is offered not to the priest as a person, but to Christ represented in him.

Since the Western Church did not have this highly developed theology of image, its concept of the ordained ministry developed along different lines. In the west the priest was seen to stand in place of the person of Christ – *in persona Christi*. At its best this can lead to a very direct and powerful experience of Christ's love and care. However, it can lead to reverence being mistakenly offered to the priest himself as a sacred person rather than to his sacramental role. This can lead to hurt and scandal when the priest is shown to be a fallible and sinful human being as much in need of God's mercy as his congregation. In practice, this difference in approach between the two Churches is a subtle difference in emphasis which goes unnoticed by most of the faithful.

There are three levels of ordination in the Byzantine Church: Bishop, Priest and Deacon. The three levels should not suggest a measure of the grace of the sacrament of Holy Orders; as if a Bishop gets all of the grace, a priest half and a deacon only a little bit. No, the fullness of the grace of the sacrament is given to each but for a different purpose. Each is graced to play a different role within the Church. This does not mean that there is an equality in honour or authority, clearly there is not, but that the Spirit will give to each of them superabundantly the grace needed for their life.

The Bishop is the chief shepherd and leader of the local Church and he stands in direct succession from the original apostles whom Christ appointed to lead the His Church. Bishops, in their own person, are the symbol of the local Church. Indeed, in Byzantine ecclesiology the Church consists of the faithful people gathered around their bishop and there can be no properly functioning Church without the bishop and his apostolic authority.

Bishops are thus first in honour among the ordained ministers because, within their diocese, they exercise the teaching authority of Christ. To them belongs the primary responsibility for proclaiming the word of God and each of the other orders is dependent for their own ministry on the authority of the Bishop. Although it may not always be evident in practice, the authority of the Bishop is not to be exercised in a domineering way, even when discipline is needed, but in a Spirit of service. The Bishop's job is to persuade the people to believe the truth, to love God and to act accordingly. As St. John Chrysostom says:

Christians above all men are not permitted to forcibly correct the failings of those who sin. Secular judges, indeed, when they have captured malefactors under the law, show their authority to be great and prevent them even against their will from following their own devices: but in our case the wrong-doer must be made better, not by force, but by persuasion. For neither has authority of this kind for the restraint of sinners been given us by law, nor, if it had been given, should we have any field for the exercise of our power, inasmuch as God rewards those who abstain from evil by their own choice, not of necessity.[135]

While the bishop is the symbol of the local Church, he is also meant to be the symbol and guarantor of the unity between the local Church and the universal Church. He does this by being in union with his brother bishops. In the ecclesiology of the Orthodox Church, all bishops are equal in authority and as brothers share the apostolic succession. When there is a dispute between two bishops it can be referred to more senior bishops, such Metropolitans or Patriarchs, so that these can act "elder brothers" in resolving the dispute, but there is (officially) no hierarchy of bishops. In the early Church the ultimate appeal in a dispute was to the Pope in Rome but this office was brought to an end in the East by the alienation and eventual split between the Latin and Byzantine Churches. The unity of the brotherhood of bishops has always been somewhat fractured but the split of the 12th century sundered the Eastern bishops from the unifying, force of the Petrine Office, the office of Peter which is claimed by the Bishop of Rome – the Pope, and simultaneously crippled the papacy's claim to speak for all Christians. Instead of being a force for unity, the papacy became a source of division as Pope John Paul II recognized in his letter *Ut Unum Sint*. After the split, the papal office developed under the exclusive influence of western theology.

The claims of the Papacy derive ultimately from the leadership position of Peter within the Apostles. The various Petrine texts which give teaching authority to the whole Church are seen as applying in a particular way to Peter who was clearly a major authority figure in the early Church. There is good evidence that Peter was finally killed by Nero in Rome where he could be presumed to be leader of that community. The Bishop of Rome can thus be seen as continuing the Petrine office. Unlike the Churches of the reform, the Orthodox Churches have known the ministry of the Petrine Office and understand its value even if they can not accept its current manifestation. They recognize that for the first 800 years of the Church's existence, it looked to Rome as a final arbiter in disputes and a guarantor of orthodoxy. The interpretation of this office is key to understanding the historic differences between the eastern and western Churches and the long, drawn out process of schism. Even the controversy surrounding the *et filoque* clause was as much a dispute over authority as over theology.

While the infallibility of the Church is part of Orthodox teaching, it is expressed in

---

135 John Chrysostom, *Treatise on the Priesthood*, Book II. Accessed in *Nicene and Post-Nicene Fathers*, Series I, Vol. IX, www.ccel.org/fathers2/NPNF1-09/npnf1-09-07.htm

Church councils where the bishops act together as brothers. In this understanding the Pope would properly be an elder brother to his brother bishops, the first in honour and respect. However, they would reject the idea that the Pope acting alone can make pronouncements that (they believe) would properly belong to a council. They also reject the worldwide immediate and ordinary jurisdiction of the Pope since they see this as cutting across the proper authority of the local bishop. They consider that this is how a king might behave but not a brother bishop – not even an elder brother. They fear that such a jurisdiction could reduce local bishops to the status of mere spokesmen for the head office – a position very much at odds with an ecclesiology based on the local Church. They also believe that such a jurisdiction puts in peril local traditions that are, in some cases, as ancient as the papacy itself.

One of the areas where the traditions of the Byzantine Church are different from those of the modern Latin Church is in the discipline of celibacy applied in the sacrament of Holy Orders. The ancient Byzantine tradition is that a married man can be ordained a priest but an ordained priest can never marry. This means that a man who wishes to be a priest can only ever marry once. If he is widowed or divorced he must remain celibate. This is similar to the discipline applied to diaconal ordination in the Roman Catholic Church. Bishops are always celibate in the Byzantine Church not so much because it is seen as desirable for the bishop to be celibate, although this is certainly true, but because it is desirable for the bishop to be a man dedicated to prayer and a life of holiness. In order to try and ensure this, Bishops are drawn from the ranks of monks who are, by definition, celibate. Those who are seen to have already given up any ambition for status or power are considered unlikely to be seduced by these things in later life. This system can be corrupted in practice but it does emphasize the central role that monasticism plays in the life and culture of the Byzantine Church.

There are two distinctly different disciplines applied in the western Church and the Byzantine discipline fits in somewhere between the two of them. The first and most ancient is that of the Roman Catholic Church which stipulates mandatory celibacy for ordinations to the priesthood (with deacons following a discipline similar to that of the Byzantine Church). The Roman Church, not always supported by the broader western Catholic Church which had married priests for a long time, has from a very early date seen great practical and theological value in a celibate priesthood. Celibacy is seen as a grace or charism essential for the exercise of priesthood. Bishops are thus always celibate since they are drawn from the body of celibate priests. The second western discipline is that of the protestant Churches where there is no link at all made between marriage and ordination and pastors are free to marry, and even remarry, as they wish.

As the early Church grew, it became impossible for the bishop to preach the word of God and to celebrate the Divine Mysteries to all of the communities under his care and local community elders were ordained by the bishop as his delegates, to perform these functions in his absence. The current priesthood fulfills this same role: the word *presbyteros* means elder. They are the delegates of the bishop who preach the gospel, celebrate the Divine Liturgy and confer the sacraments in place of the bishop. This does not mean that their priesthood is dependent on the bishop; their priesthood is a sacramental expression of the priesthood of Christ and is dependent on Him alone, but that their role in the Church derives from the role and authority of the bishop. They stand in the place of the bishop who is the true president of all the liturgies within his diocese and without the express permission of the bishop they can perform few of their priestly functions. As delegates of the bishop they also are icons of Christ in the heart of the community. Just as the local Church is the faithful people gathered around their bishop, so, on an even smaller scale, the Church is the people of God gathered around their priest. To the priest falls the normal, day to day care for the souls of God's people. He is the spiritual leader of the community and the channel through which they have access to the grace of the sacraments.

In the Byzantine Church most parish priests are married. This means that they are close to the day to day lives of their congregation. Unfortunately it also means that they, and their families, are often poor and may need to take other jobs to secure a decent income. In the past, at least, they were also often poorly educated. The practical advantages of a well educated and resourced celibate clergy were demonstrated by the great missionary effort of the western Church from the 16th century onwards, an effort which the Byzantine Church, with its emphasis on local community, has found hard to match.

The third order of the sacrament of Holy Orders is that of Deacon. While the ministry of the deacon was effectively lost to the Western Church for over a thousand years, the Eastern Church has always maintained the role of deacon as an important ministry in the life of the Church. The role of the deacon in the Church also derives from the ministry of the bishop. They are the bishop's assistants enabling him to carry out his ministry. They act as a link between the bishop and his people. They act as the bishop's ambassadors or emissaries taking his teaching to the people. They also act as the bishop's "eyes and ears" taking the concerns of God's people to their bishop. Even where the priest acts as the bishop's delegate, and the deacon thus acts as an assistant to the priest, deacons maintain their close link with their bishop.

If the deacon's are the assistants of the bishop they are also, by the grace of their ordination, heralds of the Word of God. This role is centrally exercised in the Divine Liturgy where it is the deacon who blesses the people and it is the deacon who intones the prayers on behalf of the people. Indeed, a western Christian may be surprised at extensive role of the deacon. Many of the liturgy's most visible prayers are said by the deacon with the priest only acting at crucial times in the service. In the Byzantine Church the deacon finds their central role and identity in the celebration of the Divine Liturgy.

This is at odds with the concept of a deacon as a "server of tables", someone primarily concerned with social welfare issues, which has grown in the Western Church in recent years. Due to a perceived need to curb the overreaching power of some deacons, the diaconate was reduced to a stage in the training of priests for over a thousand years in the Western Church. Its restoration was recommended by the Council of Trent in the sixteenth century but it was not until 500 years later, after the Second Vatican Council, that the diaconate was fully restored to the Catholic Church. At this time two understandings of the role of the diaconate vied with each other in the Church's deliberations. One was the ancient understanding of the Church which was very much in line with the understanding of the Byzantine Church. The other was the "server of tables" concept which was influenced by developments in the Lutheran Church and by a misreading of chapter six of the Acts of the Apostles[136]. Recent work by John Collins[137], which has concentrated on accurately translating ancient documents, has shifted the balance in favour of the ancient western (and continuing Byzantine) understanding, so that the Western Church can now echo the Eastern Church and proclaim "a deacon is never more himself than when he is wearing his dalmatic."

All three orders of the ordained ministry are required for the full celebration of the life of the Church and where one of the orders is missing, or not functioning effectively, then the life of the Church is impaired. As the western Church rediscovers the vital ministry of the deacon it will no doubt, in God's grace and time, find a new vitality to its ministry. In this process of rediscovery it may be well for the west to look to the east where the Church has a continuing 2000 year experience of the value and function of this ministry.

---

136 Gooley, A. Deacons and the Servant Myth, *The PastoralReview,* November, 2006.
137 See Collins , J.N. *Diakonia: reinterpreting the ancient sources.* Oxford University Press, Oxford, 1990. and
        Collins, J.N. *Deacons and the Church: making Connections Between Old and New.* Gracewing, Leominster, 2002.

Conclusion

A sacramental view of the world always looks towards the end times, to the 'eschaton'. It has an eschatological view. Such a view sees the universe as partial, incomplete and contingent but destined for glory. The seeds of this glory have been sown and watered by the blood of Christ whose resurrection makes present the divine destiny of all of creation. A sacramental view of the world is thus always full of hope. At no stage is this "all there is". At no stage is this "as good as it gets". For each person, life is a continuous process of growth in the Spirit of God and all the universe is in one vast process of becoming. To paraphrase St. Augustine of Hippo, we are made for God and we are restless until we find our divine destiny in Him. Indeed, many Orthodox theologians do not see even this growth into the divine as ending at death but rather as continuing into the infinity of the love of God.

In the West, eschatological consciousness and language, the awareness of the end to which the world is destined, has become so diluted in popular culture as to be almost meaningless. It even shows weakness amongst many who have been exposed partially to the biblical idea of prophecy. In the popular mind, the interpretation of revelation and prophetic utterance is largely made from a contemporary technological and media-driven perspective rather than anything biblical. Without proper theological formation in the Church, many will cite certain events like the turmoil in the middle-east, the widespread use of credit cards and computers, and the creation of the internet as signs that the coming of Jesus Christ is near. Subtly, and not so subtly, a substitute cosmology, and with it a corresponding anthropology, is being offered. With a vague awe, often inspired with the aid of the cinema, science and the media, there is a turning towards an impersonal, unchangeable cosmic monism, a philosophy which rather then seeing all of nature as graced by God and therefore sacred, sees all of the sacred as part of nature and therefore has no room for the transcendent God. In its modern form it teaches that all are but parts of one stupendous whole, whose body is nature, and God the soul. Consequently whatever *'is'* only conforms to the cosmic laws of the universal *'all'*.

The Church in the West is painfully aware of this religious-cultural situation and of its consequences. Vatican II had affirmed that man is a question to himself and only God can give him the full and ultimate answer. John Paul II noted the connection between the constant growth of an ideology in the wealthy nations characterized by pride in technical advances and a certain immanentism that lead to the idolatry of material goods, the so-called consumerism. He declared the consequences to be ominous because *'immanentism is a reduction of the integral vision of the person, a reduction which leads not to true liberation but to a new idolatry, to the slavery of ideologies, to life in constraining and often oppressive structures of this world.*' [138]

This was an echo of the concerns of the 1985 Synod of Bishops which endorsed Vatican II's affirmation of the legitimate autonomy of temporal realities in which a correctly understood secularization must be admitted, but went on to say that it was speaking of something totally different from the secularism that consists of an autonomist vision of man and the world, one which leaves aside the dimension of mystery, indeed neglects and denies it. Citing John Paul II's, *Redemptor Hominis*, the Italian commentator, Giovanni Manastra, completes the picture, declaring that

'only a new culture, a culture that is religious in a profound sense, will be able to lift the veil of ignorance and of arrogance that has, by altering the perception of the phenomenological world to the eyes of our secularized society, has generated a menacing ghost and destroyed our capacity to discern the true essence of creation'.

There has been a growing and continuing undercurrent of monism in the modern spiritual and philosophical climate for almost one hundred and fifty years, evidenced by increasing Western fascination with Hinduism (including Vedanta and Yoga) Taoism, Buddhism, Pantheism, Theosophy and Anthroposophy, Surat Shabda Yoga, Zen, and similar systems of thought, including the Occult, which explore the mystical and spiritual elements of a monistic philosophy, which in its pantheistic form identifies God with the universe and all that is in it. In short, "All is One, One is All, All is God". The implications for Christian eschatology are clear. For the last things to have any meaning at all, there needs must be a certain tension between God and creation, between the uncreated and created, between God and his human creature. Monism dissolves all these tensions and makes an eschatological view impossible. If reality is a unified whole and all existing things can be ascribed to a single concept or system, the necessary tension between created and uncreated has been cut.

'The divine mystery and greatness of the world has always been a temptation for mankind.' Mankind has perpetually abandoned God for idols, the cosmos for a profaned and secular world and the truth about mankind for its idolization. The constant temptation is to 'immanentism' a phenomenon which can assume surprising and 'unexpected forms, such as naturalism and magic, humanism and rationalism, nationalism and economism, state-worship and technology, in short every kind of idolatry'[139]

In the modern era, which has lost its faith, in which dogmatic truth has been exchanged for religion as a subjective matter of taste, there is a particular intellectual attraction in an uncompromising monistic theory of the universe. Indeed, spiritualistic monism, will always lean to semi-pantheistic mysticism

---

138 Address to the Roman Rota
139 Evgeny Lampert, *The Divine Realm: Towards a theology of the Sacraments* (London: 1943, Faber and Faber Ltd) Foreward, p 5. Hereafter, *Divine Realm*.

which exhibits only the most febrile and relative morality. As *Lifespring,* a New Age training seminar based on the monistic philosophy explains; *'The Absolute within transcends all dualities, including good and evil.'* Swami Adbhutananda, a contemporary guru, declares that *'good and evil have no absolute reality.'* He is supported by the best selling author, Deepak Chopra, in his *Seven Spiritual Laws of Success*. For Chopra, the idea that *'all is one'* really undermines any philanthrophy. If all is one flow, there are no givers or receivers. Nothing can ever be wrong since everything is equally part of the divine intelligence. The basis for morality has been dissolved. No one knows that better than Charles Manson, who asked, with a grotesque authority, *'If God is One, what is bad?'* Silva Mind Control, an influential spiritualistic self-help seminar declares that

'Everything is in some respect the universal mind and the creation of that mind... Each one of us is an idea in the universal mind. Man chooses to think of himself as a separate being... but actually we participate in this mind as an atom of water participates in the substance of the ocean.'

With radical immanentism all notions of difference, of alterity, of otherness are abolished, along with transcendence. *"Atheism is lurking somewhere at the doors"* of modernity, declared Barth. Dualism enabled modernity to constitute a world as separate from the sovereignty of God as its creator. This way dualism is the root of secularism in modernity, one of the most influential factors for the secularization of western culture. Cartesian dualism became the seed of atheism in the west, but like the lost souls in Milton's *Paradise Lost*, who flee continually from fire to ice, and from ice to fire, the continual flight is from the claustrophobia of immanent monism to the vertigo of radical dualism, each producing the other in a doomed cycle.

Monism is always the denial of this transcendant-immanent mystery and dialectic of being, its dialogical character as two-in-one, i.e. what in Christian language is called God-manhood.'[140]

The world is related to God not as His objectified equal, as a form of being as its own co-ordinated with Him, but as His living self-revelation, as His 'other one' (θατερον). It is created by God., its is God's creation. Its existence is a witness to the divine-human, theandric nature of divine being.[141]

The world is created out of the void; this means that it exists in God, and only in Him, and has no foundation of its own. It is hung over the abyss, and this abyss is 'nothingness.' Lampert declares that, *'the knowledge of 'nothingness' is one of the deepest intuitions of the creature about its creaturehood'.*[142] This creates the tension necessary for a meaningful eschatology, as well as affirming the intimate

---

140 *Divine Realm*, 12.
141 *Divine Realm*, 15.
142 Ibid.

connection between God, the world and mankind.

The ancient philosophical systems are inadequate for appreciating this vision of creation, whether they are those of Plato and Aristotle or their continuators.

They are unable to achieve a true <μεταβασις εις αλλο γενος> in which the positive unity and correlation between God and the world, as well as their ontological distinction and 'otherness' are maintained. The idea is not that of cause or movement, but of creation and creaturehood. God is not the cause of the world but its Creator, and the world is God's creation. Philosophical and theological language does not usually even notice the immense and fundamental difference between these terms. On the contrary, it is maintained that creation is but a special form of causation. Yet there is such a difference as to be virtually a contradiction.'[143]

There is no argument with his statement that *'we cannot penetrate into the depths of the life of God'*, nor with the statement that *'man is enabled to become aware of what is revealed by God himself about God's own reality'*. But Lambert then takes his reader to the edge of the precipice saying that *'To this reality belongs the creation of the world'*. Suddenly we are over the edge. He declares that the Word of God, which sounds in the Heavens, sounds also in the universe,

'what is ανα is equally κατω. The eternal image of man and of the world in man, the microcosm and the macrocosm, abides in the very heart of the hidden, triune life of God, and his inner life is revealed in the eternal image of the world and man. Such is the mystery of eternal God-manhood, the divine-human, theandric mystery of being.'[144]

This takes us to a new understanding of the sacredness of creation and establishes the creation itself as the foundation for renewed sacramental understanding. *'Created life cannot be regarded as 'caused', as a thing made- a mere product of its maker. It is not a 'thing' at all, but precisely life'*.[145] If the ideas of "efficient cause' and 'producer" are used of God and the world, God's relationship will be to extrinsic and extraneous objects. The world cannot be a sacrament of God, or a possible foundation for sacramental life, nor can man achieve or experience of God through the sacraments, if there is no living relationship between God and the other, his creation.[146]

---

143 *Divine Realm*, 44.
144 *Divine Realm*, 49.
145 *Divine Realm*, 50-51.
146 "The first sign of this divine charity must be sought in creation: ... the heavens, the earth, the waters, the sun, the moon and the stars.... Even before discovering the God who reveals himself in the history of a people, there is a cosmic revelation, open to all, offered to the whole of humanity by the Creator... There is, therefore, a divine message secretly inscribed in creation,... a sign of the loving faithfulness of God who gives his creatures being and life, water and food, light and time...From created works one ascends ... to the greatness of God, to his loving mercy." Benedict XVI, *Commentary on Psalm 135 (136)*, 9 November 2005.

When we say that the heavens proclaim the glory of God, this must not be understood in a trivial way as self- glorification or display on the part of God. The cosmos is not the theatre screen showing a movie of the divine. Rather, God *'releases, "sets free" His divine life, His divine world from out of the depths of His transcendent hypostatic being into 'otherness' and self-existence'.* When we say that God creates the world *'ex nihilo',* it means *'out of Himself, out of His own divine eternal being.'* [147] Here Lampert is entirely at one with other great theologians of the Orthodox Church, such as Fr Pavel Florensky, for whom the whole axis of creation and redemption turned upon the mystery of Golgotha, the self-offering of the God-man, Jesus.

'Golgotha was fore-ordained at the creation of the world not merely as an event in time; it also constitutes the metaphysical foundation of creation. 'It is finished', spoken by the God-man from the Cross on Golgotha embraces all being and is written across the face of the created universe....the Golgotha of God is the mysterious ground of all creation... '[148]

Contrary to dualism or reductionist monism, Christianity believes in the spiritual quality of matter. It is precisely because it is already spiritual, that matter can be the foundational element of a transcendent sacramental reality - the vehicle and revelation of the Holy Spirit. This also allows other problematic areas of human existence to be understood in a new and transfigured way, areas such as economics, sex and art.

A sacramental understanding of reality depends on the symbolic nature of creation. The symbol is a divine-human reality in which both God and his creature are operative. The meeting that occurs in a symbol is essentially a relationship of life, not of static contact, but *'living interpenetration and co-inherence.'* The symbolic power of nature is the very foundation of the sacraments and without this power there is no sacrament. However, nature cannot create the sacrament. Rent asunder through sin, nature and the whole of creation, though created holy and theandric, await God's redemptive power in Christ. Again, for Lambert, as for Florensky, all turns on Golgotha and the empty tomb. Let Lambert say it for himself:

With the coming of the God-man and Saviour Jesus Christ, with his death on Golgotha there took place a shattering and mighty exorcism of the cosmos and Nature from within: 'Great Pan has died', the demonic possession of Nature is forthwith broken, the Prince of this world is driven out, and Nature awaits her final transformation in the eschatological fulfillment.....Christ could not have fulfilled his cosmic exorcism, if Nature were not herself an ever-living witness to the Holy Spirit, whereby she cries in man and through man: Abba, Father!' [149]

---

147 *Divine Realm*, 51.
148 *Divine Realm*, 53.
149 *Divine Realm*, 116.

The patristic concept of *Metabolism* means that *'the elements of this world are translated from here to the world of the 'age to come', where God is all in all.'* The elements of Nature are *'invisibly transfigured, and while remaining ontologically themselves, become truly Spirit-bearing and are deified'.* [150] This approach still has the power today to startle Christian believers in their understanding of sacraments.

Immanent monism encloses human beings in a claustrophobic cosmos. Dualism creates an unbridgeable gulf between earth and heaven, radically dividing God and the world. However, for the Christian the Holy Spirit of God is:

that supreme Christian 'symbol', which breaks the fixed extrinsic limits and the estrangement of an objectivized world, and gives to the whole of sacramental life the quality of a dynamic all-pervading reality ... to live in the Holy Spirit is to overcome the impenetrable barriers of unilluminated, hardened, lifeless existence. [151]

The Holy Spirit is the one who allows mankind once again to breathe the clear air of restored nature, of the world that is coming, and particularly in the sacraments. The sanctification of the world, its glorification and deification in Christ's redeeming sacrifice, is only real in the coming and action of the Holy Spirit. As it is in the world, so it is in the sacraments of the Church.

'while sacraments and their power arise within the human and cosmic world of un-transfigured nature, they transcend the limits of this age and reach out to the world to come. That ray of transfiguration, that light of Mount Tabor, is not extinguished, but shines mysteriously in Christ's sacraments; and all creation seeks and longs for it. The sacrament, while it arises and is realized within this world, also reaches out to the beyond. It is a prophecy and anticipation, and thence the realization of God as 'all in all', in whom the whole cosmos is destined to become a sacrament, and man's creative, divine-human calling to be fulfilled.' [152]

---

150   *Divine Realm*, 125.
151   *Divine Realm*, 130-131.
152   Divine Realm, 139.